THE
KINGDOM
PREPPER

A BIBLICAL TIMELINE TO THE NEW HEAVEN & EARTH

DAVID RAIL STRONG

THE KINGDOM PREPPER™
©2025 by David Rail Strong
Published by The Kingdom Prepper
Austin, TX 78701
thekingdomprepper.com
thekingdomprepper@gmail.com
ISBN: 979-8-9986381-0-7 (Paperback)
ISBN: 979-8-9986381-1-4 (Hardcover)
ISBN: 979-8-9986381-2-1 (eBook)

All rights reserved. No part of this publication may be reproduced, stored in a retrieval system, or transmitted in any form by any means, electronic, mechanical, photocopying, recording, or otherwise, without the prior written permission of the publisher, except as provided by US Copyright Law.

Unless otherwise indicated, the scriptures in this book are taken from the New King James Version®. Copyright ©1982 by Thomas Nelson. Used by permission. All rights reserved.

Cover image: "New Jerusalem Ziggurat" by David Strong, created using Midjourney AI (midjourney.com) and Adobe Photoshop (adobe.com).

Cover, interior pages, and timelines designed by David Strong.

This book is dedicated to
Dr. Kent Hovind, aka "Dr. Dino,"
for his informative teachings, writings,
hospitality, and dedication to serving the Lord
while inspiring others to do the same.

Dr. Kent Hovind and David Strong (and kids).
Dinosaur Adventure Land, Repton, AL. Nov. 2023.
Creation Science Evangelism, Inc., drdino.com

CONTENTS

INTRODUCTION 1

1. THE WATCHMEN 7
    Setting Dates 7
    The Watchmen..11
    The Prophetic Calendar 13
    The 70 Weeks of Daniel 14

2. THE TRIBULATION: FALLING AWAY 19
    The 70th Week of Daniel 19
    The Tribulation...20
    The Falling Away..25
    The Antichrist..31
    The Peace Treaty...33
    The Third Temple 34
    The 7 Holy Seals 36
    The 1st Seal: The White Horse.....................................37
    The 2nd Seal: The Red Horse 38
    The 3rd Seal: The Black Horse 39
    The 4th Seal: The Pale Horse.......................................40
    Many False Prophets..41
    The 5th Seal: The Cry of the Martyrs............................42
    The Antichrist Unrestrained..44

3. THE GREAT TRIBULATION _____ 49

The Abomination of Desolation 49

The Beast 53

The False Prophet 55

The War with the Saints 57

The Mark of the Beast 60

The Number of the Beast 63

The Rise of Babylon 65

The Two Witnesses 69

The Tribulation Shortened 72

4. THE DAY OF CHRIST (RAPTURE) _____ 73

The 6th Seal: The Rapture 77

Cosmic Disturbances 78

The Voice of an Archangel 85

The Sign of Christ on the Clouds 85

The Dead Saints Raised 87

The Living Saints Raptured 89

The Judgment Seat of Christ 90

The Marriage Supper of the Lamb 93

5. THE DAY OF THE LORD: GOD'S WRATH _____ 95

The 144,000 of Israel Sealed 97

The 7th Seal: Silence in Heaven 99

The 7 Trumpet Judgments 101

    The 1st Trumpet: Vegetation Struck 102

    The 2nd Trumpet: Seas Struck 103

    The 3rd Trumpet: Fresh Waters Struck 103

    The 4th Trumpet: Heavens Struck 104

    The 5th Trumpet: Locust Army 105

    The 6th Trumpet: Euphrates Angels Released 108

    The Two Witnesses Killed & Resurrected 111

    The 7th Trumpet: God's Kingdom Proclaimed 113

    The Final Warning 115

    The 7 Bowls of Wrath 116

    The 1st Bowl: Loathsome Sore 117

    The 2nd Bowl: Sea to Blood 118

    The 3rd Bowl: Fresh Waters to Blood 118

    The 4th Bowl: Scorching Sun 119

    The 5th Bowl: Darkness & Pain 120

    The 6th Bowl: Euphrates Dries Up 121

    The Battle of Armageddon 123

    The 7th Bowl: The Final Judgment 124

    The Fall of Babylon 126

    The Second Coming of Christ (Apocalypse) 129

    Satan Sealed in the Bottomless Pit 134

    Christ's Judgment of the Nations 135

6. THE DAY OF THE LORD: THE MILLENNIUM   139

    The Earth & Jerusalem Restored 139

- The Martyrs Reign 144
- The First & Second Resurrections 145
- God's Millennial Kingdom 149
- Nations Worship the King 151
- Christ's Reign on Earth 152
- Satan Released from the Bottomless Pit 154
- Satan's Final Rebellion 156

7. THE NEW HEAVEN & EARTH — 159
- The Great White Throne Judgment 159
- The New Heaven & Earth 164
- New Jerusalem 166
- Life in Eternity 174

8. TIMELINE MODELS — 177
- Timeline Worksheet Downloads.................................178
- The 7-Day Biblical Timeline 180
- Timeline Example 183
- Top 10 Things to "WATCH!" 185

9. PREPPING FOR GOD'S KINGDOM — 193
- Start Prepping Now 197
- The Great Commission 200

APPENDICES — 201
- Timelines in this Book 201

ACKNOWLEDGMENTS

Special recognition goes to Dr. Kent Hovind, aka "Dr. Dino," whose passion, teachings, writings, and timelines inspired this book. His lifetime of dedicated research led me to the work of the late Dr. Roland Rasmussen, *The Post-Trib, Pre-Wrath Rapture: Abridged*, copyright 2014, published by the Post-Trib Research Center. I recommend his book to anyone skeptical of the post-tribulation arguments presented here, as he offers a significantly deeper examination of the published positions of prominent pre- and post-tribulation theorists. The original 1997 book is out of print; however, the 2014 ebook version is readily available.

INTRODUCTION

Biblical end-times prophecy helps us better understand God's Kingdom, His greater plan for humanity, and how His plans may unfold in our lifetime. For some, this subject matter can feel uncomfortable. For others, it motivates them to awaken and take action. This book shifts the focus from prepping for short-term survival in a troubled world to prepping for eternal life in God's Kingdom. It aims to help readers avoid being blindsided by the events of God's greater plan and to prevent them from being misled or deceived amidst the chaos.

This book offers solid theology for those seeking practical and concise answers without getting bogged down in academic debates. It also clarifies the timeline and logistics of prophetic end-times events as a basis for Bible study. It is intended for quick reading, frequent reference, and recognizing current end-times events that could begin at any moment. When one identifies that an end-times milestone has occurred, this book provides <u>timeline worksheet downloads</u> to help create a scripturally accurate countdown to the remaining prophetic events. These worksheets may also be used to evaluate other predictive timeline theories.

This book aligns with the prominent *Futurist* view of biblical prophecy, encompassing a *Dispensational Premillennialism* timeline. That mouthful means little to most, so we'll quickly break it down. Essentially, *Futurism* holds that most of the prophecies in the Book of Revelation will occur in the future, well beyond the time of their writings. *Dispensationalism* applies a specific order and structure to prophetic events and takes a more literal approach to interpreting Scripture. Finally, *Premillennialism* asserts that the return of Christ ushers in the **Day of the Lord**—a literal 1000-year period when **God's Millennial Kingdom** is established in Jerusalem, fulfilling His promises to Jewish Israel and the Christian Church.

This book agrees with the most prominent interpretations of Scripture and rejects the relatively recent notion of a "pre-tribulation rapture," popularized by 20th-century church culture. This book will demonstrate that biblical Scripture solely (and repeatedly) supports a "post-tribulation/pre-wrath rapture"—the majority view of the Church for the last 2000 years. The good news is that whether one believes in a pre-trib or post-trib rapture makes no difference to one's salvation. However, these beliefs are not theologically equal, and this book will highlight the differences and potential ramifications as we move through the prophetic timeline.

Introduction

This book will scripturally demonstrate that:

- The **Tribulation** and the **Day of the Lord** are two separate periods with different purposes.
- The 7-year **Tribulation** is inflicted by men (not God) and is divided into two equal periods: the **Falling Away** and the **Great Tribulation.**
- The **Day of Christ** *is* the **Rapture,** occurring at the end of the **Great Tribulation** (post-trib).
- The 1000-year **Day of the Lord** begins immediately after the **Day of Christ** (Rapture).
- The 1000-year **Day of the Lord** starts with 2.9 years of **God's Wrath** poured upon the Earth.
- The first 2.9 years of the **Day of the Lord** are a transition period to **God's Millennial Kingdom.**
- The **Second Coming of Christ** (Apocalypse) ends the period of **God's Wrath** at the **Battle of Armageddon.**
- The 1000-year **Day of the Lord** concludes with the **Millennium,** 997.1 years of peace under Christ's rule of **God's Millennial Kingdom.**

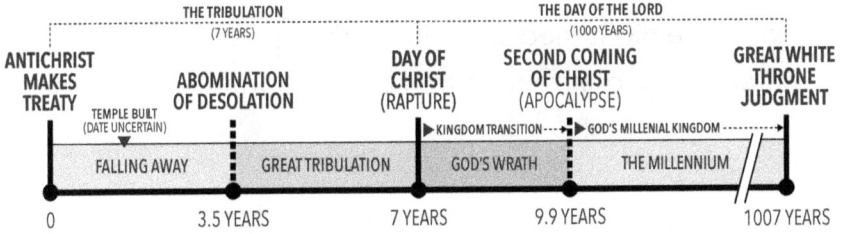

The primary audience for this book includes: 1) faithful Christian believers seeking to deepen their understanding of biblical end-times prophecy and the timeline of milestone events according to Scripture—particularly those who have never questioned the pre-tribulation rapture theory. Secondary audiences include: 2) Christian believers who have avoided studying end times due to its complexity and discomfort, 3) Christian believers who have become lax in their faith but are troubled by unfolding events in the world, 4) Christian believers who are well-versed in eschatology and remain receptive to understanding alternative perspectives, potentially addressing gaps in their own theology, and 5) curious non-Christians eager to understand the prophetic events of the end times and the broader context of God's plan for humanity as outlined in the Bible.

This book presents various opinions that may challenge the reader's preconceptions or appear contrary to modern mainstream church culture (at least in some areas). Readers are encouraged to follow along in their own Bibles, take notes, and draw their own conclusions. Even if one disagrees with some of the positions presented, it is the author's intent for them to be enlightened by alternative possibilities and strengthened in their faith. Most importantly, none of

Introduction

the positions in this book are determinative to the eternal salvation of Christian believers.

This book contains over 200 biblical scriptures from both the Old and New Testaments that directly support its content and timelines. All scriptures are taken from the New King James Version (NKJV), referred to herein as "the Bible" unless otherwise noted. Many scriptures include [bracketed] notes and <u>underlined</u> sections from the author to provide clarity and context, as well as to indicate alignment with relevant points in the body text.

Several graphic timelines are included to visually illustrate the progression of key prophetic events, with their markers emphasized in **bold** throughout the body text. Timeline worksheets and additional resources are available at thekingdomprepper.com.

Final notes: The word "rapture" means "to be carried away with great joy" and does not appear in most Bible translations. Nevertheless, it is the most recognizable term we have for this event, so this book will use it freely and often. In many instances, this book will use the biblical term "Saints" to refer to faithful believers in God, both Jewish and Christian.

Now, get ready for a seamless journey through an accurate timeline of biblical end-times events...

CHAPTER 1
THE WATCHMEN

SETTING DATES

This book does not predict the exact dates for the prophetic events of the end times, and many scriptures clarify that only God knows when these events will occur. However, the Bible does offer insight into how some events will begin, the order in which they take place, and their duration. Faithful believers in Christ are told to be watchful of the *"times and seasons,"* as if these events could begin at any moment—which is sound advice for any potential storm.

"But of <u>that day and hour no one knows</u>, not even the angels of heaven, <u>but My Father only</u>." [–Jesus]

Matthew 24:36 (NKJV).

When Jesus said this, He was living as a man and, undoubtedly, He answered truthfully from His mortal perspective. Indeed, He could have petitioned God (the Father) for the answer, but He chose not to seek or share that information with His disciples. From His throne in Heaven today, He surely knows the hour. The preceding verse is among the most quoted when discussing the timing of Jesus' return. The argument goes, *"We won't know the day or the hour, so there's no way of knowing if Jesus will come tomorrow or in a thousand years."* While it's true that we won't know the exact *"day and hour"* of His return, this is truly an argument for *imminency*—that He could return at any moment. Jesus continues His thought by relating the pre-flood days of Noah to His return...

"But <u>as the days of Noah were</u>, so also will the <u>coming of the Son of Man be</u> *[Day of Christ (Rapture)]*. **For as in the days before the flood, <u>they</u>** *[the unbelievers]* **were eating and drinking, marrying and giving in marriage, until the day that <u>Noah</u>** *[the Saints]* **entered the ark, and** *[the unbelievers]* **<u>did not know until the flood</u>** *[God's Wrath]* **came and <u>took them all away</u>, so also will the coming of the Son of Man be."** *[–Jesus]*

Matthew 24:37–39 (NKJV).

Jesus emphasizes that it was the UNBELIEVERS who were caught unprepared and suffered God's wrath—not the faithful believers who were saved (raptured) by building, preparing, and entering the ark at the appointed time. Jesus explains that this is how it will be at the time of His return. The unbelievers will be caught by SURPRISE, but the believers should remain prepared and EXPECT His return at the appointed time. The unbelievers will suffer **God's Wrath,** and the believers will be raised to everlasting life. So, while we may not know the exact *"day and hour"* of His return, faithful believers are certainly to watch the *"times and the seasons"* and live in readiness. We see a similar message in Paul's letter to the church at Thessalonica…

But concerning the <u>times and the seasons</u> *[of events to come],* **brethren, <u>you have no need that I should write to you</u>. For you yourselves <u>know perfectly that the day of the Lord</u>** *[God's Wrath]* **<u>so comes as a thief in the night</u>** *[to the unbelievers].*

---

1 Thessalonians 5:1–2 (NKJV).

Paul specifies *"the day of the Lord,"*—not the **Day of Christ** (Rapture)—clarifying that it's **God's Wrath** that overtakes the unbelievers, just as in the story of Noah. The point remains consistent: UNBELIEVERS will be surprised and suffer **God's Wrath**—not faithful believers. Paul even rebukes his brethren because they *"know perfectly that the day of the Lord [God's Wrath] so comes as a thief in the night"* for the unbelievers, but not for them. This verse is often cited to promote an *imminent* surprise return of Christ for His believers, but it conveys the opposite. This point is driven home in Paul's next verse...

For when <u>they</u> [the unbelievers] **say, "Peace and safety!" then <u>sudden destruction comes upon them</u>,** as labor pains upon a pregnant woman. **And <u>they shall not escape</u>** [God's Wrath].

1 Thessalonians 5:3 (NKJV)

Paul clarifies it is the UNBELIEVERS who will be lulled into a false sense of *"peace and safety"* before facing **God's Wrath.** In contrast, he advises his brethren to remain watchful for Jesus' return...

But you, brethren [in Christ], **are <u>not in darkness</u>** [worldly ignorance]**, so that this Day should overtake you as a thief. You are all <u>sons of light</u> and <u>sons of the day</u>** [children of God]**. We are <u>not of the night nor of darkness</u>. Therefore <u>let us not sleep</u>** [ignoring the signs]**, as others do, but <u>let us watch and be sober</u>** [for His return].

1 Thessalonians 5:4–6 (NKJV).

Paul concludes the passage by contrasting the awareness of believers who are *"of the light"* with that of unbelievers who are *"of the darkness."* While unbelievers *"sleep,"* faithful believers are called to *"watch and be sober"* for Jesus' return.

In the next section, Jesus instructs His believers to pay attention and *"Watch!"* for His return. The Bible does not provide specific dates; however, it does include a few durations that we can use to measure the intervals between certain milestone events. Once we clearly identify an initiating event, we can formulate a countdown to the remaining milestones. Our goal is to confirm prophetic events as they happen. We can also attempt to *predict* the timing of initiating events, but that's more of an exercise to help keep us sharp.

THE WATCHMEN

Although studying Bible prophecy may be uncomfortable for some, Jesus instructs His faithful believers to keep watch and prepare for His return…

"<u>Watch therefore</u>, for you do not know <u>when the master</u> of the house <u>is coming</u> [Christ's return]–in the evening, at midnight, at the crowing of the rooster, or in the morning–lest, coming suddenly, he find you sleeping [unprepared]. And what I say to you, I say to all: <u>Watch!</u>" [–Jesus]

Mark 13:35–37 (NKJV).

Jesus commands His believers to proactively "Watch!" so that they are not caught unprepared by the season of His return. The Old Testament prophet Ezekiel describes *"watchmen"* who are appointed to listen to God's word, recognize impending dangers, and sound the warning to both believers and unbelievers. If the people hear the watchman's words but choose not to heed his warning, then the responsibility for their fate lies with themselves...

---

when he [the watchman] **sees the sword coming** upon the land, if he **blows the trumpet** and **warns the people**, then whoever **hears the sound** of the trumpet **and does not take warning**, if the sword comes and takes him away, his blood shall be **on his own head** [for not heeding the warning].

Ezekiel 33:3–4 (NKJV).

However, if the watchman recognizes impending dangers and fails to warn the people, he will be held responsible for their fate. The passage continues...

But if the watchman sees the sword coming and does not blow the trumpet, and the people are not warned, and the sword comes and takes any person from among them, he is taken away in his iniquity [unredeemed wickedness]; **but his blood I will require at the watchman's hand** [the watchman is responsible].

Ezekiel 33:6 (NKJV).

Therefore, it is essential to warn the unbelievers, as they must be given every opportunity to recognize the truth of God's larger plan and repent to receive salvation before being overtaken.

THE PROPHETIC CALENDAR

The Bible was written using the PROPHETIC CALENDAR, sometimes referred to as the "Bible Calendar" or the "Temple Calendar." The Hebrew Calendar is based on a LUNAR YEAR consisting of 354.36 days. Today, we use the more commonly known Gregorian Calendar (derived from the Roman Julian Calendar introduced by Julius Caesar in 45 BC), which is based on a SOLAR YEAR of 365.25 days, resulting in an almost 11-day difference between the two. Interestingly, when averaged, Solar and Lunar Years yield the PROPHETIC YEAR, which comprises a tidy 360 days (12 months of 30 days each). This is the Prophetic Calendar referred to in Scripture whenever days, months, and years are mentioned. Therefore, this book employs the Prophetic Years specified in Scripture for its discussions and timelines, unless otherwise noted. In some cases, we will reference SYMBOLIC YEARS as a biblical storytelling device, such as 1 day = 1 year or 1 day = 1000 years, illustrated by this example....

...with the Lord <u>one day is as a thousand years</u>, and a thousand years as one day.

2 Peter 3:8 (NKJV).

THE 70 WEEKS OF DANIEL

The prophetic events leading up to the **Millennium** are foretold in the Old Testament book of Daniel. While in captivity in Babylon, Daniel prayed for the restoration of his people, the Jews, to their land, Jerusalem, which the Babylonians had besieged. Soon after, the angel Gabriel personally delivers the message to Daniel that God has heard his prayers and will answer them. However, Gabriel goes beyond Daniel's original request and describes when the ultimate restoration of Jerusalem and the Jewish people will occur in relation to other events...

Seventy weeks [seventy-sevens] ***are determined*** *[by God]*
For your people [the Jews] ***and for your holy city*** *[Jerusalem],*
To finish the transgression,
To make an end of sins,
To make reconciliation for iniquity,
To bring in everlasting righteousness,
To seal up vision and prophecy,
And to anoint the Most Holy [Jesus Christ].
[–The Angel, Gabriel]

Daniel 9:24 (NKJV).

Gabriel uses Symbolic Years here (1 day = 1 year) to convey his prophecy, meaning that 1 week refers to 7 years. In many biblical translations, the word

1. The Watchmen

"sevens" replaces "weeks" to clarify that Daniel is referring to "a group of sevens." Therefore, *"seventy weeks"* becomes *"seventy-sevens"* (70 x 7 = 490 years). Gabriel continues...

Know therefore and understand,
That from the going forth of the command
To restore and build Jerusalem
Until Messiah the Prince, [arrives in Jerusalem]
There shall be seven weeks and sixty-two weeks; [7 + 62 = 69]
The street shall be built again, and the wall, [the 7 weeks]
Even in troublesome times. [the 62 weeks]
[–The Angel, Gabriel]

Daniel 9:25 (NKJV).

The first *"seven weeks"* (7 x 7 = 49 years) represents the restoration period to rebuild Jerusalem. The subsequent 62 weeks (62 x 7 = 434 years) signify *"troublesome times"* for the Jews. Now, here's where it gets interesting. At the end of the 69th week—483 years after Emperor Artaxerxes commanded King Nehemiah to rebuild the wall of Jerusalem—Jesus rode a colt into Jerusalem and presented Himself as the King (Messiah) to the Jewish people, exactly as Gabriel foretold in Daniel's prophecy. Christians now refer to that day as "Palm Sunday." Upon entering Jerusalem, Jesus mourns over the city—and specifically the Temple—because it would be destroyed some 37 years later at the hands of the Romans. He then gives the primary reason for its destruction: the failure of the Jewish Pharisees to *"know the time"* of His coming....

---

*"... and they [the Romans] **will not leave in you** [Jerusalem] **one stone upon another, because <u>you did not know the time of your visitation</u>** [the Lord's coming]." [–Jesus]*

Luke 19:43–44 (NKJV).

Had the Pharisees followed Daniel's prophecy and Gabriel's explicit instructions to *"Know therefore and understand,"* they may have recognized Jesus as their Messiah. Once again, Jesus seems to warn us to *"Watch!"* for the season of His return, lest we fail to recognize Him or be deceived BEFORE He arrives. This lesson is full of consequences. Because they were ignorant of His timing, within the span of one week (7 days), the Jewish Pharisees would:

- reject Jesus as their King (on behalf of all Jews),
- accuse Him of false crimes,
- hand Him over to the Roman authorities,
- demand that He be tortured and crucified (though He was found innocent),
- celebrate His death, and
- deny His resurrection.

Because God's chosen people (the Jews) did not receive Jesus, Daniel's 70 weeks were paused at the end of week 69, leaving one week (7 years) before the *"anointing of the Most Holy"* (Jesus). Numerous examples exist of biblical prophecies with pauses or interruptions, so this is not a stretch of Scripture

Jesus was most likely crucified in 33 AD, so it's been almost 2000 years since that pause. That's the period we're in now, called the **Church Age** or the "Time of the Gentiles." This is when God grafts in the Gentiles (non-Jews) to carry Jesus' *"gospel of the kingdom"* to the world before the end of days…

"And this [Christ's] <u>gospel of the kingdom</u> will be preached in <u>all the world</u> [by the Church/Gentiles] as a witness to <u>all the nations</u>, and <u>then the end will come.</u>" [–Jesus]

Matthew 24:14 (NKJV).

Daniel's last remaining week (7 years), often referred to as **"The 70th Week of Daniel,"** could begin at any moment, officially starting the countdown to the **Day of Christ** (Rapture) and the **Day of the Lord** when **God's Millennial Kingdom** is restored on Earth.

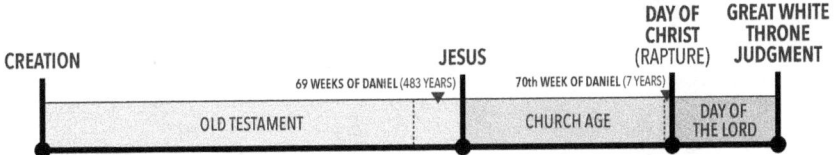

The Saints (believers in Christ) should not fear the end times, no matter how frightening they may seem. For the Saints, the end times represent the *"good news"*—the very definition of the Gospel of Christ. For unbelievers (those who ignore or reject Jesus), the end times are extremely bad news.

If you'd like to understand (right now) how close we could be to the prophetic events of the end times, you're welcome to skip to Chapter 8: The 7-Day Biblical Timeline and return here afterward to read about the details of the events to come.

CHAPTER 2
THE TRIBULATION: FALLING AWAY

THE 70TH WEEK OF DANIEL

The last week (7 years) of Daniel's prophecy, known as the **70th Week of Daniel,** begins with a specific event: the Antichrist brokers a 7-year peace **Treaty** *"with many."* Presumably, this **Treaty** includes Israel, as it provides for the rebuilding of the Jewish **Third Temple** on the Muslim-controlled Temple Mount in Jerusalem. The Antichrist breaks this **Treaty** halfway through the 7 years by defiling the new **Temple** and making it desolate for 2300 days, an event referred to as the **Abomination of Desolation.**

Then he [the Antichrist] ***shall*** <u>***confirm a covenant***</u> *[peace treaty]* <u>***with many***</u> ***for*** <u>***one week***</u> *[7 years]; **But*** <u>***in the middle of the week***</u> *[3.5 years]* ***he shall bring an*** <u>***end to sacrifice***</u> ***and offering*** *[defile the Third Temple]*

Daniel 9:27 (NKJV).

The **70th Week of Daniel** is commonly referred to as the **Tribulation.** The previous Scripture indicates that this period of **Tribulation** is divided *"in the middle of the week"* at 3.5 years. The first 3.5 years are scripturally referred to as the **Falling Away** (this chapter), while the last 3.5 years are termed the **Great Tribulation** (the next chapter).

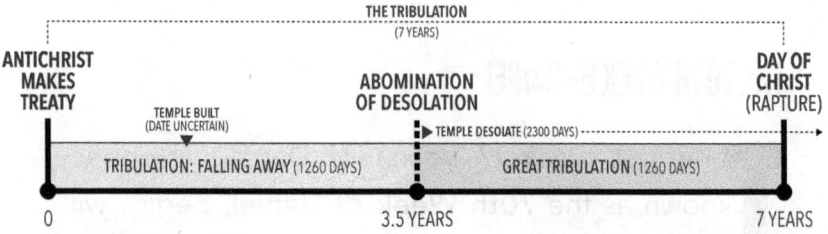

THE TRIBULATION

The timeline above illustrates that the **Day of Christ** (Rapture) of the Church Saints occurs AFTER the **Tribulation.** This is known as a post-tribulation or "post-trib" rapture and is a primary tenet of this book. If one adopts the notion of a "pre-trib" rapture, they believe that Jesus removes His faithful Saints from Earth BEFORE the **Tribulation** begins. Whether one believes in a pre-trib or post-trib rapture makes no difference to one's eternal salvation; however, these views are not theologically equal. A post-trib rapture has been the majority view of the Church for the past 2000 years, though a sampling of

2. The Tribulation: Falling Away

mainstream church teachings today may give the opposite impression. A pre-trib rapture is a comforting idea that first arose in the mid-1800s. Unfortunately, there is no biblical Scripture to support it—unless one confuses (or intentionally conflates) *"tribulation"* with *"wrath,"* which the scriptures carefully separate. Let's start with the **Tribulation.**

A "tribulum" is a primitive threshing board used to press and grind stalks to separate the grains from their husks and chaff, distinguishing the valuable from the worthless. John the Baptist uses this metaphor to describe what it will be like for the believers and unbelievers during the 7-year **Tribulation…**

---

*"… He [Jesus] will <u>baptize you with the Holy Spirit and fire</u>. His winnowing fork is in his hand to <u>clear his threshing floor</u> and to <u>gather the wheat</u> [faithful believers] **into his barn** [heaven], but he will <u>burn up the chaff</u> [unbelievers] with unquenchable fire."*
[–John the Baptist]

Luke 3:16–17 (NKJV).

John the Baptist lays it all out here. Humanity's faith must be thoroughly tested; those who are found faithful will be gathered and saved. The rest will fall away to the threshing floor to be burned in everlasting fire. So, what does Jesus say about His believers enduring the 7-year **Tribulation?**

"These things I have spoken to you, that <u>in Me you may have peace</u>. In the world <u>you will have tribulation</u>; but <u>be of good cheer</u>, I have <u>overcome the world</u>." [–Jesus]

John 16:33 (NKJV).

Jesus assures the Saints that they may take comfort in Him, but He also warns that they *"will have tribulation"* in the world (from men), and it gets worse...

"Then <u>they</u> [men] will <u>deliver you up to tribulation</u> and <u>put you to death</u>, and <u>you will be hated by all nations</u> [men everywhere] <u>for my name's sake</u>." [–Jesus]

Matthew 24:9 (NKJV).

Jesus does NOT say His followers will escape *"tribulation"* nor that He will punish them. He states that their persecution will be delivered by *"all nations"* (men everywhere) specifically FOR their belief and professed faith in Him. This should not come as a surprise, as the Apostles certainly faced tribulation, enduring persecution, imprisonment, and torture in the years following Jesus' resurrection. To assume that Christian believers today would be immune from such treatment would be naive.

Data from Open Doors (opendoorsus.org) indicates that 380 million Christians face high levels of

2. The Tribulation: Falling Away

persecution and discrimination worldwide today. This number includes 4,476 Christians who were murdered in 2024 specifically for their professed faith in Christ. It's clear that Christians HAVE SUFFERED and continue TO SUFFER *"tribulation"* at the hands of men, but they do not endure *"wrath"* from God. Prominent biblical examples include Noah's family, preserved from the flood, and Lot's family, evacuated before the destruction of Sodom and Gomorrah. In both stories, **God's Wrath** afflicted only the wicked unbelievers. Clearly, there is a distinction between *"tribulation"* and *"wrath."*

The Greek word for *"tribulation"* is *"thlipsis,"* which can also signify affliction or trouble, but it never means *"wrath,"* and Scripture never confuses the two. In fact, in virtually every use in the New Testament, *"thlipsis,"* (or its verbal cognate, *"thlibo"*) describes persecution suffered by Christians at the hands of men, the Antichrist, or Satan. *"Wrath"* is translated from two Greek words, *"thumos"* and *"orge,"* depending on severity. When either is referring to **God's Wrath,** it is applied solely to the wicked in every instance.

Therefore, it is essential to understand that the torment of the **Tribulation** period *(thlipsis)* is NOT to be conflated with the period of **God's Wrath** *(thumos, orge).* The first half of the **Tribulation** (the

Falling Away) illustrates what humanity inflicts upon itself without restraint from God. The second half of the **Tribulation** (the **Great Tribulation**) represents what the Antichrist imposes on humanity without restraint from God. In simple terms, "tribulation" is delivered by men and the Antichrist, while "wrath" is delivered solely by God...

For God <u>did not appoint us</u> [the Saints] to [His] <u>wrath</u>, but to obtain salvation through our Lord Jesus Christ,

---

1 Thessalonians 5:9 (NKJV).

Pre-tribulationists have utilized the preceding verse to advocate for their pre-trib theory for decades by conflating *"tribulation"* with *"wrath."* However, when *"wrath"* is appropriately defined and any confusion with *"tribulation"* is removed, this verse supports a post-trib/pre-wrath rapture. We see a similar confusion applied to Jesus' words (transcribed by John) to the church in Philadelphia...

"Because you have have kept My command to <u>persevere</u> [endure patiently], **I also will keep you** [My church] **from the <u>hour of trial</u>** [testing], **which shall come upon the whole world, to test <u>those who dwell on the earth</u>** [unbelievers]." [-Jesus]

Revelation 3:10 (NKJV).

2. The Tribulation: Falling Away

This is another popular verse used to promote a pre-trib rapture of the Church; however, this verse does not mention or refer to the **Tribulation** period. *"The hour of trial"* is translated from the Greek word *"pirasmos,"* which means "to test." In this context, it refers to "testing or adversity sent by God," equating it with **God's Wrath.** This is confirmed by the phrase *"Those who dwell on the earth,"* which appears throughout the Book of Revelation solely in reference to the unsaved who rebel against God and worship the Beast. This verse simply reaffirms the universal belief (both pre-trib and post-trib) that UNBELIEVERS will face **God's Wrath,** while the Saints of the Church will not. It is unrelated to the **Tribulation.**

In summary, the Saints endure **Tribulation** from men and the **Great Tribulation** from the Antichrist, but they will not experience **God's Wrath,** which begins immediately AFTER the **Day of Christ** (Rapture). We will explore this distinct separation and its scriptural cross-references further down the timeline.

THE FALLING AWAY

We've established that Christians are persecuted worldwide and suffer *"tribulation"* at the hands of men even today. However, the 7-year **Tribulation** represents the final *"apostasia"* (apostasy) of the **Church Age,** during which many believers abandon their faith in Christ—a great **Falling Away** at the last hour—a specific period distinct from any past periods of "*tribulation.*" If the post-tribulationists are incorrect and experience a pre-trib rapture at this point, we can all share a good laugh in Heaven. However, if the pre-tribulationists are wrong and no pre-trib rapture occurs, they may face a difficult time that they have not considered and may be completely unprepared for. It's the difference between preparing for a storm that doesn't materialize and being caught unprepared in a storm that could be deadly.

The Bible warns that many faithful Saints, potentially millions, will *"fall away"* and succumb to the Antichrist's social and economic system during the 7-year **Tribulation.** The most tragic fall may be those who believe in a pre-trib rapture. Many faithful Saints could *"fall away"* because their church, books, movies, and podcasts promised they would be raptured out BEFORE the **Tribulation** began. So, this is not just an esoteric discussion of differing theological opinions. Considering the catastrophic risk of millions of Christians abandoning their faith in the final hour of the **Church Age,** we must at least consider that a pre-trib rapture theology could be one of the greatest cons of the *"father of lies."*

"Let no one deceive you," Paul warns the Church of Thessalonica as he clarifies their misunderstanding

2. The Tribulation: Falling Away

regarding the *imminence* of Christ's return—that He could come back at any moment—dismissing the foundational pillar of a pre-trib rapture...

Now, brethren, concerning <u>the coming of our Lord Jesus Christ</u> and our <u>gathering together to Him</u> [the Rapture], we ask you, not to be soon shaken in mind or troubled, ... as though the <u>day of Christ</u> [the Rapture] had come. <u>Let no one deceive you</u> by any means; for <u>that Day</u> [the Day of Christ (Rapture)] <u>will not come unless the falling away</u> [the first half of the Tribulation] <u>comes first, and the man of sin is revealed</u>, the son of perdition, [the midpoint of the Tribulation]

2 Thessalonians 2:1–3 (NKJV).

This passage is one of the most critical in Bible prophecy, and it supports a post-trib/pre-wrath rapture: the *"falling away"* and the *"man of sin is revealed"* (both events of the **Tribulation**) must occur BEFORE *"the day of Christ"* (the **Rapture**).

Pre-tribulationists argue that this is a translation error—that these two events must occur before the **Day of the Lord** (which they combine with the **Tribulation**), an event that a pre-trib rapture would theoretically precede. Fine, but that contradicts their argument for *imminency*. The **Rapture** cannot be *imminent* if two conditions must precede it. We'll look at more distinctions between the **Tribulation** and the **Day of the Lord** later in the timeline.

So, what does the first half of the **Tribulation** look like in the world? At first, life is relatively good. It's a period of (false) peace as the Antichrist rises in influence by securing the **Treaty** that no one else could. Most of the world embraces a global governance body and relinquishes their privacy in the name of safety and security. Sound familiar? They are conditioned to view ongoing wars, viral epidemics, and manufactured disasters as acceptable conditions for humanity and do not perceive anything unusual about the increasing street violence and social chaos. They even support or participate in the oppression, as long as it's directed at those they strongly oppose or disagree with, as we've seen in recent years.

Their ignorance of biblical Scripture and their "normalcy bias" prevent them from noticing that anything abnormal is happening. They believe that things continue as they always have—at least since Christ walked the Earth 2000 years ago. Sin remains normalized—even encouraged—and the secular world enjoys the expansion of the "freedoms" afforded to them. They persist in serving their own interests and ridicule those who warn them of Jesus' return and God's impending judgment…

2. The Tribulation: Falling Away

> *...knowing this first: that <u>scoffers will come in the last days</u>, walking [behaving] <u>according to their own lusts</u> [sinful pursuits] and saying, "Where is the promise of His [Jesus'] coming? For since the fathers [prophets] fell asleep [died 2000 years ago], all things continue as they were from the beginning of creation."*
>
> 2 Peter 3:3–4 (NKJV).

Peter writes that *"scoffers will come in the last days,"* taunting believers by asking, *"Where is the promise of His coming?"* This could serve as a direct message to those who believed in a pre-trib rapture that did not take place. Those Saints may feel ashamed, forsaken, or, worse, deceived into thinking that the **Rapture** occurred and that they were intentionally "left behind."

As conditions worsen, more Saints begin to *"fall away."* Many (perhaps millions) of previously faithful Saints succumb to the social and economic pressures of a global health and commerce system initiated by the Antichrist. They are compelled to replace their faith in God as a means of survival.

In Matthew 24, Jesus warns of wars, epidemics, earthquakes, false prophets, persecution, famines, and betrayals. However, He also instructs His followers not to be troubled, for these events *"must come to pass"* to fulfill God's plan...

"And you will hear of <u>wars and rumors of wars</u>. See that you are <u>not troubled</u>; for all these things <u>must come to pass</u> [to fulfill God's plan] but <u>the end is not yet</u>. For nation will rise against nation, and kingdom against kingdom. And there will be famines, pestilences [epidemics], and earthquakes in various places. All these are <u>the beginning of sorrows</u>." [–Jesus]

Matthew 24:6–8 (NKJV).

Jesus does not promise His followers that they will avoid suffering during the **Tribulation.** Instead, He encourages them to be patient, for *"the end is not yet,"* and they have more challenges to face as these events are just *"the beginning of sorrows."* However, He does promise peace and salvation for those who maintain their faith in Him...

*"And because **lawlessness** [violence and tyranny] **will abound** [during the Tribulation], **the love** [compassion] **of many will grow cold. But <u>he who endures to the end shall be saved</u>."** [–Jesus]*

Matthew 24:12–13 (NKJV).

Jesus promises His Saints, *"who endure to the end"* of the **Tribulation** (or die trying) will be raptured and receive eternal salvation at its conclusion. He also promises great rewards for those who rise to overcome their adversity and continue practicing His faithful works...

And he <u>who overcomes</u> [maintains their faith], and <u>keeps My works until the end</u>, to him <u>I will give power over the nations</u> [in God's Millennial Kingdom]–'<u>He shall rule them</u> with a rod of iron [under Christ's authority]; They shall be dashed to pieces like the potter's vessels' [for not obeying authority]–as I also have received from My Father; and I will give him <u>the morning star</u> [the fellowship of Jesus].

Revelation 2:26–28 (NKJV).

These passages clarify that: 1) the **Rapture** is not *imminent*; 2) the Saints are present during the **Tribulation;** 3) the suffering faced by the Saints during the **Tribulation** is not from God—it's from man; and 4) the Saints will be greatly rewarded for enduring and overcoming the challenges of the **Tribulation.** These truths all confirm a post-trib/pre-wrath rapture.

THE ANTICHRIST

So, who—or what—is the Antichrist? The Bible mentions the term "Antichrist" in only four verses. Many movies have depicted the birth and childhood of the Antichrist, such as "The Omen" (1976), but this portrayal attempts to equate the Antichrist with Jesus in the context of a divine birth. The Bible does not contain any reference suggesting that Satan's progeny is destined to be born into this world.

Instead, the Antichrist is a fully mortal man, chosen from the populace and ultimately possessed by the spirit of Satan himself. There are always numerous potential Antichrist vessels placed in various positions to be elevated—or replaced—as Satan deems necessary. It's quite possible that we have observed some level of this practice throughout history and can recall a few likely candidates.

Furthermore, the term "antichrist" applies to anyone who denies that Jesus is Lord and Christ, anyone who stands against Christ, or even anyone who desires nothing to do with Christ. The Apostle John tells us that there are *"many antichrists"*...

Little children, *[new believers in Christ]* **it is the last hour; and as you have heard** *[in prophecy]* **that <u>the Antichrist is coming</u>, even now <u>many antichrists have come</u>, by which we know that it is the last hour** *[nearing the end of days].*

---

1 John 2:18 (NKJV).

Here, John likely refers to prominent individuals who are (or have been) representatives of Satan—actively carrying out his bidding. Most respected theories indicate that the Antichrist is a significant world figure with multiple leaders or institutions under his authority. This could pertain to a key role in a government, religion, or consortium, such as a

2. The Tribulation: Falling Away

president, prime minister, or figurehead. Regardless of who this person is and their position, it's more crucial to focus on the spirit of the Antichrist rather than on the individual. Any time we see anti-human agendas or practices, we are looking at the spirit of the Antichrist and should watch for his emergence.

THE PEACE TREATY

The first event to officially initiate a prophetic countdown of the end times is the 7-year peace **Treaty** brokered by the Antichrist. *"Wars and rumors of wars"* in the Middle East involving Israel, for instance, create an opportunity for the Antichrist to intervene and negotiate a peace **Treaty**—likely including discussions to rebuild the **Third Temple** in Jerusalem. In 2025, we can observe this scenario developing, although the conflict will probably escalate as more countries become involved to achieve the desired outcome.

Scripture does not tell us when the peace **Treaty** will occur, but it seems imminent. There's also a chance that the **Treaty** could be made quietly and announced later or that the terms for rebuilding the **Third Temple** could be part of a more extensive negotiation. That's to say, even if we're made aware of its existence, the exact date of agreement or ratification of the **Treaty** could be fuzzy.

THE THIRD TEMPLE

The first temple, Solomon's Temple, stood for 404 years before the Babylonians destroyed it in 423 BC. The second temple was rebuilt in 349 BC and lasted for 419 years before the Romans destroyed it in AD 70. As of 2025, the Jewish people have not had a primary temple for 1955 years, which is understandable considering that the current State of Israel was not established until 1948.

Today, two Muslim mosques, the Dome of the Rock and Al Aqsa (built around AD 700), stand on the Temple Mount in Jerusalem, strategically positioned to prevent the Jewish people from rebuilding their temple in its original location. However, it's possible that the first Jewish temple was situated west of the Eastern Gate, on an empty 10-acre plot slightly north of the mosques today. Considering the Temple Mount's size of 37 acres, there appears to be ample room on-site for both mosques and the **Third Temple** today. However, construction on this site is politically sensitive and would require cooperation among many interested parties, including the Arab League of Nations, Israel, and Jordan, to name a few. Permission to rebuild the **Third Temple** on the Temple Mount would demand more political will than legal authority and process.

2. The Tribulation: Falling Away

Given that Scripture indicates that prominent political and religious leaders will follow the Antichrist, he will occupy an unprecedented position to negotiate this sensitive proposal. Jewish teachings suggest that their coming Messiah will usher in the construction of the **Third Temple** and that its final completion will prove his divinity. This could explain how the Jewish people might initially come to accept the Antichrist as their Messiah.

The construction of the **Third Temple** does not provide a specific point on the timeline for measurement; however, such a highly publicized event would confirm that the peace **Treaty** has indeed been ratified and that the 7-year **Tribulation** has begun. The time from the date of the **Treaty** to the **Temple's** desolation is 3.5 years. Is that enough time to build the new temple from scratch? You bet your bagels it is! The Temple Institute in Jerusalem has been working for decades, assembling plans, pre-cut materials, and artifacts to build and adorn their new **Temple**—all of which are viewable today at templeinstitute.org. Construction could be completed rapidly—likely within 6 months.

The purification ceremony is the first step in rebuilding the **Third Temple.** It requires the sacrifice and burning of a flawless red heifer (a perfectly red, unblemished cow) whose ashes are used to purify the

Jewish priests for their service in the new **Temple**. This ceremony is conducted off-site and in direct view of the future temple's entrance. In September 2022, five perfect, unblemished red heifers arrived in Israel (from Texas) and are of sacrificial age in 2025. An appropriate site for the purification ceremony, located on the adjacent Mount of Olives, was purchased in 2010 and offers a direct view of where the two previous temples stood, just beyond the Eastern Gate. From a timeline perspective, the only obstacle to rebuilding the **Third Temple** is negotiating permission to do so on the desired site.

THE 7 HOLY SEALS

In the Book of Revelation, Jesus reveals prophetic visions to His servant, John. Early in the book, John describes a heavenly vision of Jesus opening 7 holy scrolls by breaking the seals that secure them. As we will detail later, God's "seal" is a signet of protection. Breaking these 7 Holy Seals removes certain protections that God holds over the Earth. As discussed, the suffering during the **Tribulation** is inflicted by the tyranny of men (and ultimately Satan), unrestrained by God. The 7 seals are broken sequentially, with the first 4 seals releasing the famed "Four Horsemen of the Apocalypse," representing CONQUEST, WARFARE, FAMINE, and DEATH. These riders appear to be released during the first half of the **Tribulation**—the **Falling Away**—marking the countdown to the end times and, ultimately, the Apocalypse.

THE 1ST SEAL: THE WHITE HORSE

Jesus breaks the seal on the 1st Holy Scroll, releasing the white horse and its rider, symbolizing CONQUEST. The rider wears a crown and holds a bow...

And I looked, and behold, a <u>white horse</u>. He who sat on it had a <u>bow</u> [absent arrows]; and a <u>crown</u> [authority] was <u>given to him</u>, and he went out <u>conquering</u> and to conquer.

Revelation 6:2 (NKJV).

There has been some confusion about this 1st white horse and the white horse that Jesus rides down from the heavens almost 10 years later at the **Second Coming of Christ** (Apocalypse) toward the **Battle of Armageddon.** Jesus wears *"many crowns;"* this rider wears a single crown that *"was given to him,"* presumably by God as permission to carry out the events that *"must come to pass."* Jesus carries the sword of judgment; this rider carries a bow but no arrows. Jesus leads the armies of Heaven; this rider is alone. Jesus smites His enemies at the final **Battle of Armageddon;** this rider is followed by three other riders with greater destructive power. Jesus ushers in a time of peace and blessings; this rider ushers in a time of warfare, famine, and death. In summary, this rider is a counterfeit of Christ—the Antichrist—and he brings a false peace.

Since the **Tribulation** begins with the peace **Treaty,** the 1st seal might be broken BEFORE that event to provide time for the Antichrist to gain power. He may hold a worldly position of authority but does not directly control an army or weapons of war (he has a bow but no arrows). For example, he could be a leader in the UN, NATO, the UK royal monarchy, the Vatican, or a global corporation. All of these would be positions of authority in highly influential organizations, yet they do not formally possess or control an army or weapons.

THE 2ND SEAL: THE RED HORSE

Jesus breaks the 2nd seal, releasing the red horse and its rider, symbolizing WARFARE…

---

*Another horse, <u>fiery red</u>, went out. And it was <u>granted to the one who sat on it to take peace from the earth</u> [make war], **and that people should kill one another** [mass violence]; **and there was <u>given to him a great sword</u>** [weapons/armies].*

Revelation 6:4 (NKJV).

The rider of the red horse wields *"a great sword,"* representing the authority that *"was given to him"* to unleash mass chaos and violence. This unrest could signify a regional conflict, such as a territorial dispute, escalating tensions between nations, or even a full-scale world war. Unlike the rider of the white horse, this rider does not appear to embody a single individual or nation. Instead, his appearance removes God's restraint on humanity, granting them full power to obliterate peace and destroy one another.

THE 3RD SEAL: THE BLACK HORSE

Jesus breaks the 3rd seal, releasing the black horse and its rider, symbolizing FAMINE…

---

*…and behold, a <u>black horse</u>, and he who sat on it had a pair of [trading] <u>scales in his hand</u>. And I heard a voice in the midst of the four living creatures saying, "A quart of wheat [about one loaf of bread] **for a denarius** [one day's wages], **and three quarts of barley for a denarius; and do not harm the oil and the wine."**

Revelation 6:5–6 (NKJV).

The rider of the black horse carries scales representing trade and currency. The example provided in Scripture for the price of wheat (bread/food) would equate to at least ten times the average for us today—that's 1000% inflation! This may sound impossible, but we've seen this many times before in collapsed nations where their fiat (paper) currency is devalued to near worthlessness. This type of global inflation is devastating, especially for developing countries. The costs could rise much higher in wealthier countries, and restrictions in the supply chains would be catastrophic.

THE 4TH SEAL: THE PALE HORSE

Jesus breaks the 4th seal, releasing the pale horse and its rider, symbolizing DEATH; its pale, grayish-green color resembles decaying flesh...

---

*So I looked, and behold, a <u>pale horse</u>. And the name of him who sat on it was <u>Death</u>, and <u>Hades</u> [the realm of the dead] **followed with him**. And [unbridled] <u>**power was given to them**</u> over a <u>**fourth of the earth**</u>, to kill with sword, with hunger, with death, and by the beasts of the earth.*

Revelation 6:8 (NKJV).

This final rider brings about widespread loss of life, partly due to the effects of the previous three horses, which represent CONQUEST, WARFARE, and FAMINE. With a population of 8 billion, a *"fourth of the Earth"* means that 2 billion people could die in just a few short years. The phrase *"beasts of the earth"* conjures a particularly gruesome idea, and it's uncertain whether this inclusion alludes to familiar wildlife or to more exotic and mythological creatures.

MANY FALSE PROPHETS

After the devastations released by the Four Horsemen, the world is exhausted and primed for rescue. Its leadership has faltered, creating a vacuum that allows many *"false prophets"* to emerge, each with the promise of saving their people and solving the world's problems…

"For <u>false christs</u> and <u>false prophets</u> will rise and show signs and <u>wonders to deceive</u>, if possible, even the elect [Saints]." [–Jesus]

Mark 13:22 (NKJV).

Here's a short list of groups that have been waiting for their saviors for a very long time:
- The Christians are waiting for the return of their Lord, Jesus Christ.
- The Jews are waiting for their Messiah.
- The Muslims are waiting for their 12th Imam (the Mahdi).
- The Hindus are waiting for their Krishna.
- The Buddhists are waiting for their 5th Buddha.
- The Cultists and secret societies are waiting for their Enlightened One.

Each group believes their savior has arrived, but all are misled, potentially as part of an elaborate deception. Even some devoted Saints are deceived due to their limited understanding of Scripture and eagerness for Jesus's return. This confusion paves the way for the rise of the Antichrist as a singular solution for all nations and religions. He enters the world stage like a white knight to end the turmoil and suffering that no one else could. Much of the world now follows and venerates the Antichrist as their leader and savior, granting him ultimate authority. He now leads the one-world government and religion.

THE 5TH SEAL: THE CRY OF THE MARTYRS

Jesus breaks the seal of the 5th Holy Scroll, revealing "the souls" of the Saints who were martyred for their professed faith in Him during the **Church Age** and up to this moment in the **Tribulation**...

When He [Jesus] **opened the fifth seal, I saw under the altar** *[in Heaven]* **the souls of those who had been slain** *[before and during the Tribulation]* **for the word of God** *and for the* **testimony** *which they held. And they cried with a loud voice, saying, "How long, O Lord, holy and true, until* **You judge and avenge our blood** *on those who dwell on the earth [with your wrath]?" Then a* **white robe** *was given to each of them, and it was said to them that they should* **rest a little while longer** *until both the number of*

2. The Tribulation: Falling Away

*their fellow servants and their brethren [in Christ], **who would be killed as they were, was completed** [the end of the Tribulation].*

Revelation 6:9–11 (NKJV).

Some readers of this book are likely included in the voices John hears in his vision—let that sink in. This passage is among the strongest in support of a post-trib/pre-wrath rapture. When the martyred Saints cry for **God's Wrath** (Judgment) to avenge their deaths, they are told to *"rest a little while longer"* until AFTER the last of the **Tribulation** Saints are *"killed as they were."* Thus, more Saints will be killed (by men) during the remainder of the 7-year **Tribulation,** and the martyred Saints AWAIT for **God's Wrath** (Judgment) to be released upon the world to *"avenge their blood,"* thus initiating the **Day of the Lord.**

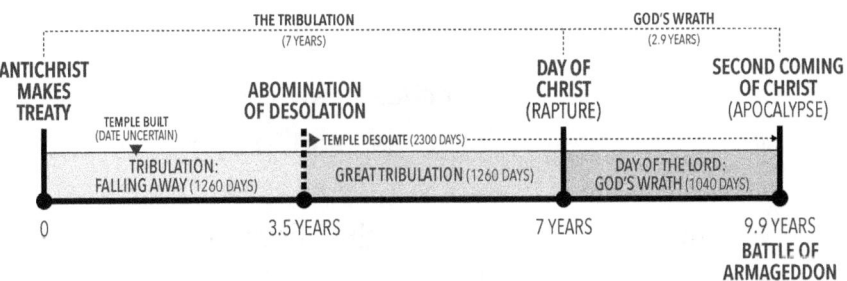

This Scripture confirms that: 1) the **Tribulation** and **Day of the Lord** are two separate events, 2) the

Saints will endure *"tribulation"* from men, but not *"wrath"* from God, 3) the first 5 seals are not *"wrath"* because **God's Wrath** has not yet begun. These truths eliminate the need for a pre-trib rapture to protect the Church from *"wrath"* and reinforce the prevailing belief of a post-trib/pre-wrath rapture. **God's Wrath** will begin AFTER the breaking of the 7th seal (post-**Rapture**) and will be poured out in the **Day of the Lord**—not during the **Tribulation** (the **70th Week of Daniel**).

Breaking the 5th seal removes the last remaining protections that the Lord has established over the **Tribulation** Saints, leaving them completely exposed to the Antichrist during the **Great Tribulation,** which is about to start. By this time, the Antichrist has solidified his political power and spiritual authority.

THE ANTICHRIST UNRESTRAINED

Since the *Garden of Eden,* Satan's actions have been restrained by God. He moves freely on Earth, creates confusion, spreads influence, and propagates lies, but is prohibited from physically interacting with men without permission. We see this restraint repeatedly demonstrated in the oldest book of the Bible, Job. In a conversation with God, Satan petitions to afflict Job's possessions to test the authenticity of his faith.

God grants this request but forbids Satan from inflicting any physical harm on Job...

And the Lord said to Satan, "Behold, all that he has is in your power; only <u>do not lay a hand on his person</u> [his physical body]."

Job 1:12 (NKJV).

After losing everything he owned and many of the people he loved, Job still maintained his faith in God. Frustrated, Satan further petitions to afflict Job physically. God grants the request but forbids Satan from killing Job...

And the Lord said to Satan, "Behold, he [his physical body] **is in your hand, but <u>spare his life</u>."**

Job 2:6 (NKJV).

After enduring severe physical afflictions, Job still upheld his faith in God and imparted a powerful lesson to the Saints—especially to those who will live to endure the **Tribulation...**

"...Shall we indeed accept [only] **good from God, and shall we not accept adversity?" In all this Job did not sin with his lips** [did not curse God for his afflictions].

Job 2:10 (NKJV).

During the second half of the **Tribulation**—the **Great Tribulation**—the Antichrist is unleashed upon the world without restraint from God. Not even the Saints are shielded from Satan's rage after the 5th seal is broken, thus removing God's final line of protection over them. The **Great Tribulation** marks a time of Satan's unrestrained fury, and the Saints become public enemy number one. They will be *"given into his hand"* during the **Great Tribulation**...

---

*...Then <u>the saints</u> shall be <u>given into his hand</u> [the Antichrist] **For a <u>time and times and half a time</u>** [3.5 years].*

Daniel 7:25 (NKJV).

This verse explicitly states that the Saints WILL endure the **Tribulation**—specifically the 3.5 years of the **Great Tribulation**. Just as God permitted Job's faith to be tested, so too is the faith of the **Tribulation** Saints. This is their moment to persevere. The greatest rewards in the universe await those who maintain their faith, reject false gods, witness to others, and proclaim Jesus Christ as their Lord and Savior in the face of the worst adversaries. The **Tribulation** is a difficult period but merely a moment in the scale of eternity, one that we can reflect on proudly, should we persevere, as Paul reminds us...

2. The Tribulation: Falling Away

*...we also glory in tribulations [times of trouble], **knowing that tribulation produces perseverance; and perseverance, character; and character, hope.***

Romans 5:3 (NKJV).

Breaking the 5th seal clears the way for Satan to advance his plan to the next phase—the **Great Tribulation.** This is the moment he has orchestrated for centuries.

CHAPTER 3
THE GREAT TRIBULATION

THE ABOMINATION OF DESOLATION

The second half of the **Tribulation** (the **Great Tribulation**) begins when the Antichrist breaks his 7-year peace **Treaty** *"with many"* (after 3.5 years). He erects an idol of himself in the **Third Temple** and proclaims himself to be God...

[the Antichrist] **who opposes and <u>exalts himself</u> above all that is called God or that is worshiped, so that <u>he sits as God</u> in the** *[third]* **<u>temple of God</u>** *[in Jerusalem],* **showing himself that he is God.**

2 Thessalonians 2:4 (NKJV).

This act is called the **Abomination of Desolation** and marks the start of the **Great Tribulation...**

"Therefore when you see the '<u>abomination of desolation</u>,' spoken of by Daniel the prophet, standing in the <u>holy place</u> [the Temple] [...] **For <u>then there will be great tribulation</u>**..." *[–Jesus]*

Matthew 24:15, 21 (NKJV).

This is a milestone event on the prophetic timeline and probably the FIRST FIRM DATE we can use to begin counting the 3.5 Prophetic Years (1260 days) until the **Day of Christ** (Rapture).

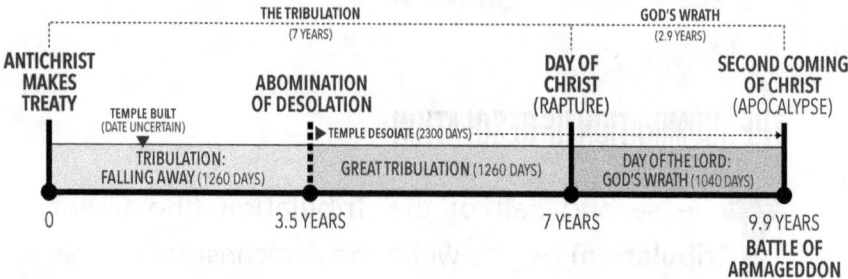

The actions of the Antichrist render the **Third Temple** desolate for 2300 days—1040 days past the end of the **Great Tribulation** and the **Day of Christ** (Rapture)...

... *"How long will the vision be, <u>concerning the daily sacrifices</u> [in the Temple] and the <u>transgression of desolation</u>, the giving of both the sanctuary and the host to be <u>trampled underfoot</u>?" And he [the angel] said to me, "For <u>two thousand three hundred [2300] days; then the sanctuary shall be cleansed."*

Daniel 8:13–14 (NKJV).

These 2300 days of *"desolation"* may only apply to the Jews because the Antichrist and his followers continue to *"trample"* the sanctuary grounds during this time, possibly using the **Temple** for his unholy

3. The Great Tribulation

purposes. The *"sanctuary shall be cleansed"* after 2300 days following the **Second Coming of Christ** (Apocalypse) and the **Battle of Armageddon,** when the Antichrist and his armies are ultimately destroyed. The culmination of these events marks the end of **God's Wrath** at 1040 days.

While it may sound arcane to many today, animal sacrifices will resume when the **Temple** is rebuilt as an act of obedience to the Lord in repentance for sin (and PETA will likely lose their minds). After the Antichrist's forces storm the **Temple** and *"take away the daily sacrifices,"* an abominable object *"stands"* in the Holy Place, likely an image or idol representing the Antichrist...

And <u>**forces shall be mustered by him**</u> *[the Antichrist]*, **and they shall <u>defile the sanctuary fortress</u>** *[Third Temple]*; **then they shall <u>take away the daily sacrifices</u>, and <u>place there the abomination of desolation</u>** *[in the Holy Place].*

Daniel 11:31 (NKJV).

There is a vigorous debate that Daniel's prophecy already occurred in 167 BC, when the Greek King Antiochus Epiphanes raided the second Jewish temple and sacrificed a pig on a makeshift altar to Zeus, thus defiling it and leaving it desolate for two years until it could be appropriately cleansed and sanctified. While these actions of King Antiochus align with some of Daniel's prophecies, he certainly did NOT *"make an end of sins," "bring in an everlasting righteousness,"* or *"anoint the Most Holy,"* to name a few (see Chapter 1: The 70 Weeks of Daniel). Therefore, we can view the actions of King Antiochus as foreshadowing the coming Antichrist. Pattern is a powerful device that we frequently observe in Scripture—especially in prophecy. When we recognize that something has happened before, we better accept the possibility that it could happen again.

"So when you see the 'abomination of desolation,' spoken of by Daniel the prophet, standing where it ought not [in the Temple sanctuary]" **(let the reader understand), "then let those who are in Judea** [region of Jerusalem] **flee to the mountains."** [–Jesus]

Mark 13:14 (NKJV).

When the **Temple** sanctuary is desecrated, Jesus warns the people of the region to evacuate quickly. At this moment, the Antichrist is fully revealed, leaving no doubt about his identity and purpose. As a result of this deception, many Jews turn to the Lord in shame and accept Jesus as their true Messiah and eternal Savior.

3. The Great Tribulation

THE BEAST

In short, the Beast is the Antichrist. In the last chapter, we discussed his rise to INFLUENCE in brokering the peace **Treaty** that initiated the **Tribulation.** His rise to POWER occurs when Satan controls him through spiritual possession. He is the deceiver who sits at the head of all tables. For many religions, he is the savior they have longed for—the one who unites them into a one-world religion. For those lacking spiritual grounding and seeking answers in the secular world, he is their Superman.

He performs incredible signs and wonders—nothing short of miracles in the eyes of the world. He employs clever words and flattery that stimulate their egos and subconscious minds. He is masculine, charismatic, and speaks with authority. He is exalted for bringing peace to the world, but this is his ultimate deception. In the book of Revelation, the Beast is depicted in wild imagery…

Then I stood on the sand of the sea. And I saw <u>a beast rising up out of the sea</u>, having <u>seven heads and ten horns</u>, and on his horns <u>ten crowns</u>, and on his heads a blasphemous name

---

Revelation 13:1 (NKJV).

The "sea" symbolizes worldly rebellion and chaos, and the Antichrist is empowered to emerge from the populace. His role likely resembles that of a POLITICAL leader with *"seven heads and ten horns,"* where *"ten crowns"* signify his allied kingdoms and influence. We are provided with numerous details and characteristics to identify the Beast, but one striking detail is that he survives a head wound (inflicted by a sword) so severe that he seems to have been resurrected from death...

And I saw one of his heads as if it had been <u>mortally wounded</u>, and <u>his deadly wound was healed</u>. And all the <u>world marveled</u> [at his apparent resurrection] **and <u>followed the beast</u>.**

Revelation 13:3 (NKJV).

This may be the moment when Satan spiritually enters the Antichrist, reviving his dead (or dying) body to imitate the resurrection of Christ. Upon awakening, he is possessed by Satan himself and under his direct control. The Antichrist is now referred to as *"the Beast"* and is *"given authority"* to make war during the 3.5 years of the **Great Tribulation,** likely initiated by the breaking of the 5th seal...

And he [the Beast] **was given a mouth speaking great things and blasphemies, and he was <u>given authority</u> to continue** [make war] **for <u>forty-two</u> [42] months** [3.5 Prophetic Years/1260 days].

Revelation 13:5 (NKJV).

THE FALSE PROPHET

A few verses later, we learn of *"another beast coming up out of the earth."* The imagery suggests a religious leader known as *"the False Prophet"*...

Then I saw <u>another beast coming up out of the earth</u>, [the False Prophet] and he had two horns like a lamb and spoke like a dragon. And he exercises <u>all the authority of the first beast in his presence</u>, and causes the earth and those who dwell in it to <u>worship the first beast, whose deadly wound was healed</u>.

Revelation 13:11–12 (NKJV).

The role of this second beast is to endorse and entice the world to worship the first Beast. He exercises the same authority and performs the same miracles *"in the sight of the beast,"* implying he derives his power from proximity to the Beast...

He [the False Prophet] <u>performs great signs</u> [false miracles], so that he even makes fire come down from heaven on the earth in the sight of men. And <u>he deceives those who dwell on the earth</u> [the unbelievers] by those signs which he was <u>granted to do in the sight of the beast</u>, telling those who dwell on the earth [the unbelievers] to <u>make an image</u> [idol] to the beast who was wounded by the sword and lived.

Revelation 13:13–14 (NKJV).

Indeed, those without discernment marvel at the "miracles" of the False Prophet. He falsely claims that the Beast is "resurrected" from death—proving his godliness—and instructs the deceived to *"make an image"* of the Beast for worship. The False Prophet is *"granted power to give breath to the image,"* thus bringing it to life, either spiritually or artificially...

He [the False Prophet] **was <u>granted power to give breath</u>** [life] **to the <u>image</u>** [idol] **<u>of the beast</u>, that the image of the beast should both <u>speak and cause as many as</u>** [everyone who] **<u>would not worship the image of the beast to be killed</u>.**

Revelation 13:15 (NKJV).

While this "living" idol may represent a spiritual manifestation, one cannot ignore the possibility of a sentient robot or projected *"image"* with artificial intelligence (AI). The strange notion that it will know who does *"not worship the image"* implies an AI system capable of tracking behavior on a global scale—not only that of those present in the room. It also possesses the ability to *"speak and cause"* (or perhaps order) the deaths of those who refuse to worship it, again, on an apparent global scale. This echoes King Nebuchadnezzar's decree to execute anyone who refused to worship his golden idol.

3. The Great Tribulation

> *"Then if anyone says to you, 'Look, here is the Christ!' or 'There!' <u>do not believe it</u>. For <u>false christs</u> and <u>false prophets</u> <u>will rise and show great signs and wonders to deceive</u>, if possible, even the elect [the Saints]. See, <u>I have told you beforehand</u>." [–Jesus]*
>
> Matthew 24:23–25 (NKJV).

Jesus warns us not to believe in *"false prophets"* or to be deceived by their *"great signs and wonders,"* again appearing to foretell a great deception. Saints who are deceived bear responsibility for their gullibility, as they have been warned *"beforehand."* Resisting deception is a test, making it essential to be grounded in Scripture, lest one be deceived and held accountable at the **Great White Throne Judgment.**

THE WAR WITH THE SAINTS

> *It was <u>granted to him</u> [the Beast] **to <u>make war with the saints</u>** [Christians] **and to <u>overcome them</u>** [for 3.5 years]. And <u>authority</u> was given him <u>over every tribe, tongue,</u> and <u>nation</u> [the world].*
>
> Revelation 13:7 (NKJV).

The Beast is *"granted"* the authority to *"make war with the saints and to overcome them"* during the 3.5 years of the **Great Tribulation** (as noted in verse 13:5 in the last section). Logically, the Saints must be

PRESENT during the **Great Tribulation** if the Beast is to wage war against them and overcome them. Since a pre-trib rapture would negate this possibility, this verse provides strong evidence for a post-trib/pre-wrath rapture.

The **Great Tribulation** represents a challenging period for many, yet the Christian Saints are seen as public enemy number one. Their faith is strained and tested to the utmost degree. They face physical, spiritual, and economic attacks from global governance, a one-world religion, and the Beast's digital identification and commerce system. As outcasts, they are easily identifiable because they lack the *"mark of the Beast"* when scanned, which could reasonably occur at the crowd level in any public area. They are likely arrested, taken to re-education camps, and ultimately killed if they continue to pledge their loyalty to Jesus...

"Then <u>they</u> [men in the Beast's system] will <u>deliver you up to tribulation and kill you</u>, and you will be <u>hated by all nations for My name's sake</u>." [–Jesus]

Matthew 24:9 (NKJV).

This is their offer: *"Deny Jesus as Lord, and we'll let you live."* This is the crucial test for Saints during the **Great Tribulation.** Saints should NEVER deny

3. The Great Tribulation

their faith and belief in Jesus—even in the face of death or torture. This is a tough message for many churches today: *"Join us, and you'll be hated, tortured, and killed."* It's not exactly the marketing approach that fills pews. It's no wonder that many churches—especially the larger ones—have adopted a pre-trib rapture position. Even churches that adhere to the majority view of a post-trib/pre-wrath rapture are adept at keeping that part quiet—at least when trying to attract new members.

"Also I say to you, <u>whoever confesses</u> [their faith in] Me before men, him the <u>Son of Man</u> [Jesus] also will <u>confess before the angels of God</u>. But he who <u>denies Me before men</u> will be <u>denied before the angels</u> of God." [–Jesus]

Luke 12:8–9 (NKJV).

And if confessing their faith in Him *"before men"* leads to the ultimate punishment, Jesus tells His followers, *"do not worry beforehand,"* and provides guidance on what to do—and what not to do...

"But when they <u>arrest you and deliver you up</u> [for punishment], <u>do not worry beforehand, or premeditate what you will speak</u>. But whatever [word] is given you in that hour, <u>speak that;</u> for it is <u>not you who speak</u>, but the <u>Holy Spirit</u>." [–Jesus]

Mark 13:11 (NKJV).

So when Saints are persecuted and facing severe punishment—even death—they must remain faithful and at peace, with clear minds, so that the words of *"the Holy Spirit"* can speak through them as a witness to others. The executions of the Saints are likely public (as they have been throughout history), making their testimonies carry significant weight for those who hear them. The stronger their conviction, the more powerful their inspiration to others.

THE MARK OF THE BEAST

This end-times prophecy is among the most widely recognized and over-analyzed. Confusion begins with a simple translation discrepancy in a key verse from Revelation. Examine this verse closely in the original King James Version (KJV)...

And he causeth all, both small and great, rich and poor, free and bond, to <u>receive a mark</u> in their <u>right hand</u>, or in their <u>foreheads</u>:

Revelation 13:16 (KJV).

Now, compare the same verse in the New King James Version (NKJV)...

He causes all, both small and great, rich and poor, free and slave, to <u>receive a mark</u> on their <u>right hand</u> or on their <u>foreheads</u>,

Revelation 13:16 (NKJV).

3. The Great Tribulation

Did you notice the difference? The word *"in"* was changed to *"on"* twice. Nearly all modern Bible translations have adopted this change. The Greek word in question is *"epi,"* which can be translated as either *"in"* or *"on."* It's a minor distinction in most cases, but *"in their forehead"* differs significantly from *"on their forehead."* The next verse completes the sentence…

…and that <u>no one may buy or sell</u> except <u>one who has the mark or the name</u> of the beast, <u>or the number</u> of his name.

Revelation 13:17 (NKJV).

As a noun, a *"mark"* refers to a visible sign or symbol, such as a tattoo in this context, which makes the most sense when found *"on their forehead"* or hand. In a pre-technological society, this interpretation appears to be the only logical option. With modern technology, we have more options to consider.

In recent decades, the theory that *"the mark"* refers to a microchip implanted *"in the hand"* has gained traction as this technology became a reality. Nowadays, having our pets "microchipped" is commonplace. People may now volunteer to have microchips implanted *"in their hand,"* with the chip's functions extending far beyond simple identification.

A tiny microchip can store or unlock an individual's complete health history, medication prescriptions, passports, and even banking data, allowing purchases to be made with a palm swipe. Some have also associated cell phones with this verse since they are held *"in the hand."*

"In their forehead" is somewhat more complicated but is rapidly becoming a reality. Neuralink's "brain implant chips" (neuralink.com) are undergoing human trials, and the results are impressive. To bring the conversation full circle, tattoos can now integrate microchip technology into the ink, offering the same digital identification as an implant while providing a surface *"mark"* on the skin for visual identification—wow!

Regardless of the form that *"the mark"* takes, look for a companion device, like a phone app, for banking and purchasing with a new one-world digital currency. *"The mark"* probably also functions as a digital ID and health passport, verifying vaccination status for travel, attending live events, and other freedoms we've always taken for granted. These systems began to be implemented in 2020 during COVID-19 and are progressing well in some countries. When geo-location and AI behavioral analysis are incorporated, subject movements aren't just tracked—they're predicted.

3. The Great Tribulation

This one-world system likely emerges in the first half of the **Tribulation.** Its implementation and widespread adoption require time and must be established by the **Great Tribulation** to be fully effective. Scripture is clear: participating in the Beast's one-world system equates to professing loyalty to Satan, though many may not fully grasp this consequence...

... *"If anyone <u>worships the beast and his image</u>, [participates in his system] and <u>receives his mark</u> on his forehead or on his hand, he himself <u>shall also drink of the wine of the wrath of God</u>, ..."*

Revelation 14:9–10 (NKJV)

The social pressure to adopt this technology is intense, and the penalty for refusal is severe. Those who refuse *"the mark"* are labeled as enemies of the state and are subjected to harassment, arrest, and even death. However, even if such a mark were made mandatory globally, it does not mean it can (or will) be enforced everywhere.

THE NUMBER OF THE BEAST

The previous passage expanded to include *"the <u>mark</u> OR the <u>name</u> of the beast, OR the <u>number of his name</u>."* When the Beast is revealed by defiling the **Third Temple,** we will surely know his name. But what is the number of his name?

> ***Here is <u>wisdom</u>*** *[take note]*. ***Let him who <u>has understanding</u>*** *[insight and intelligence]* <u>***calculate the number of the beast***</u>***, for it is <u>the number of a man</u>: His number is <u>666</u>.***
>
> Revelation 13:18 (NKJV).

This is another well-known prophecy surrounded by wild speculation in movies and pop culture. "*The mark*" could be a number, barcode, or QR code. Additionally, this number seems to indicate the identity of the Beast himself, either as a hint before he is revealed during the **Abomination of Desolation** or as confirmation afterward.

"*The number of a man*" is traditionally 6 in the Bible. God gave life to Adam on the 6th day, and 6 falls just short of 7—the number of perfection attributed to God. Three 6s may represent a bastardization of God's Holy Trinity, comprised of Satan, the Beast, and the False Prophet. Others consider the word "*calculate*" as an instruction to decode. One theory suggests that his first, middle, and last names each consist of 6 letters (three sets of 6).

Another consideration is the spelling of his name. Each letter of the Hebrew alphabet has a corresponding numeric value, as do some Greek and Roman letters. Additionally, we may not be searching for a proper name—it could represent a position, title, or another type of identification.

THE RISE OF BABYLON

The rise of "*Babylon*" is a central theme in end-times biblical prophecy. She unfolds in the shadows of many other events and does not occupy a specific point on our timeline, though it aligns well with this section of the book. Numerous scriptural references trace back to Daniel's prophetic visions and carry through Revelation—all employing vivid imagery and symbolism that require some speculation…

And I saw a <u>woman</u> sitting on a <u>scarlet beast</u> which was full of names of blasphemy, having <u>seven heads and ten horns</u>.

Revelation 17:3 (NKJV).

This is the same "*beast*" we saw a few sections back, "*rising up out of the sea, having seven heads and ten horns, and on his horns ten crowns,*" which refers to the Antichrist and the 10 future kingdoms (nations) under his influence in the last days…

"The <u>ten horns</u> [with crowns] which you saw are <u>ten kings</u> who have received no kingdom as yet, but <u>they receive authority for one hour</u> [a short period] <u>as kings with the beast</u>. These are <u>of one mind</u>, and they will <u>give their power and authority to the beast</u>."

Revelation 17:12–13 (NKJV).

There is much speculation about who these 10 nations are, with the most prominent views pointing to a revived Roman Empire (perhaps via the Vatican City in Rome) and a combination of European and various Middle Eastern countries united by their disdain for Israel. These 10 nations could also include superpowers such as Russia and China. The number 10 might also symbolize completeness, suggesting that most or all modern nations (at some level) are allied to form a one-world government body, similar to NATO. These 10 kings *"receive authority"* for a brief period, implying that the Beast installs each of them in a global coup. In return, they *"give their power and authority to the beast."*

And <u>on her forehead a name was written</u>: MYSTERY, BABYLON THE GREAT, THE MOTHER OF HARLOTS AND OF THE ABOMINATIONS OF THE EARTH. [...] And the <u>woman</u> whom you saw <u>is that great city</u> which <u>reigns over the kings of the earth</u>."

Revelation 17:5, 18 (NKJV)

The woman symbolizes *"Babylon the Great,"* the one-world empire of nations united and controlled by the Beast. The name *"Babylon"* serves as a biblical stereotype for the enemies of God and His people (the Jews), while the term *"Harlot"* is a metaphor for those who adhere to a false religion. Thus, this allied empire stands as an adversary of Israel, promoting a false, one-world religion with the Beast as its central figure. The Beast coerces religious conformity, and the woman (empire) entices the nations with promises of wealth and prosperity. Together, they captivate the world and form a rebellion to rise against God and His people. We won't know the name of this empire until it's officially established, so we'll continue to refer to it as "Babylon" and use feminine pronouns when discussing her.

During the 7-year **Tribulation,** POLITICAL Babylon ascends as a global economic power, trading in luxury items, precious metals, jewels, fine commodities, and agricultural products. Her delicacies entice the nations and strengthen their alliances, encouraging them to partake in her wealth. She soon becomes the jewel of the world—man's finest kingdom in history—and all profit from her affluence.

RELIGIOUS Babylon emerges as a new one-world belief system, constructed on the foundations of established religions, deceiving their followers and drawing in new-age converts. Speculation about which religions may make up this one-world abomination is varied, though many concur it will involve Catholicism (Christianity) and Islam. Oddly, a sect of Judaism may be the third primary member of this interfaith disgrace since they accepted the initial (false) peace **Treaty** brokered by the Antichrist to build their **Third Temple.** Regardless of its identity or the assembly of its parts, it is likely to be an inclusive religion that embraces a pluralistic view of God, ultimately leading its followers to the worship of the Beast. (See Chapter 8: Top 10 Things to "WATCH!": #6 The Abrahamic Family House, and #7 The Abraham Peace Accords.)

---

*I saw the woman [Babylon the Great], **drunk with <u>the blood of the saints</u> and with <u>the blood of the martyrs of Jesus.</u>***

Revelation 17:6 (NKJV).

This verse unambiguously refers to the Saints of the **Tribulation,** who are explicitly killed for their faith in Christ and their refusal to take *"the mark of the Beast"* and worship his image. If the Saints were removed in a pre-trib rapture, then they would not be present for *"the woman"* to drink *"the blood of the saints and ... martyrs."* Unless one argues that these Saints are new converts—an unlikely premise given the account of events from the 5th seal—this verse confirms that the Saints are present to endure suffering (and death) during the **Tribulation,** further supporting a post-trib/pre-wrath rapture. We'll see the martyred Saints again in the next chapter.

3. The Great Tribulation

THE TWO WITNESSES

At the beginning of this chapter, we learned that the **Abomination of Desolation** renders the **Third Temple** desolate, and it is *"trampled underfoot"* for 2300 days by the Antichrist and his followers.

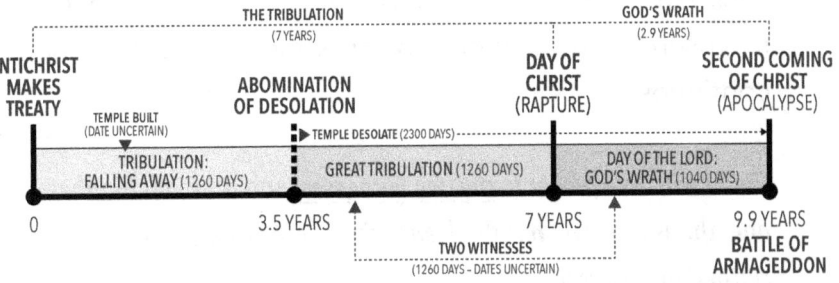

These 2300 days extend 1040 days past the end of the **Great Tribulation** and the **Day of Christ** (Rapture), marking the **Second Coming of Christ** (Apocalypse) and the **Battle of Armageddon** on our prophetic timeline. At some point within these 2300 days, the court outside the temple is given to the Gentiles (non-Jewish nations) for 42 months…

"But leave out <u>the court which is outside the temple</u>, and do not measure it, for <u>it has been given to the Gentiles</u> [non-Jews]. And they will <u>tread the holy city underfoot</u> for forty-two [42] months [1260 days]."

Revelation 11:2 (NKJV).

At this time, God sends His **Two Witnesses** to Jerusalem to proclaim the gospel of Christ while much of the world chooses to worship and believe the lies of the Beast. Their ministry lasts 1260 days—the same 42 months that the Gentiles are permitted to occupy the outer court of the **Third Temple.** The **Two Witnesses** are *"clothed in sackcloth,"* a historical representation of grief and repentance. The passage continues...

"And I will give power to <u>my two witnesses</u>, and they will <u>prophesy</u> one thousand two hundred and sixty [1260] days [42 months], <u>clothed in sackcloth</u>."

Revelation 11:3 (NKJV).

The popular theory suggests these **Two Witnesses** are the Old Testament prophets, Enoch and Elijah. Both are well-suited for the role and share a unique qualification...

And as it is appointed for men <u>to die once</u>, but after this the [Great White Throne] <u>judgment</u>, ...

Hebrews 9:27 (NKJV)

Men are appointed *"to die once,"* and the only two individuals in history known to have escaped physical death are Enoch and Elijah, as God took each of them directly to Heaven. They prophesy for 1260 days and are subsequently killed. This fulfills their mission, and they will have died only once. During a time when the Beast is unleashed on the world without God's restraint, these **Two Witnesses** teach the gospel of Christ with impunity. Anyone who attempts to harm them is met with abrupt and painful consequences...

These [Two Witnesses] **are the** *two olive trees* **and the** *two lampstands* **standing before the God of the earth. And** *if anyone wants to harm them,* *fire proceeds from their mouth* [God's word as fiery judgment] **and** *devours their enemies.* **And if anyone wants to harm them,** *he must be killed* **in this manner.**

Revelation 11:4–5 (NKJV).

The **Two Witnesses** are the only individuals exempt from the Beast's rage—and they revel in that liberty. They perform miracles, preach the gospel of Christ, and drive hardened unbelievers crazy with their unapologetic boldness and relentless rebukes. Every action they take creates a spectacle; we can imagine their viral presence on social media. If they were a movie, it would be titled "Grumpier Old Prophets."

THE TRIBULATION SHORTENED

"For then there will be <u>great tribulation</u>, such as has not been since the beginning of the world until this time, no, nor ever shall be. And <u>unless those days were shortened no flesh would be saved</u>; but <u>for the elect's sake</u> [the Saints] those days [of Great Tribulation] <u>will be shortened</u>." [–Jesus]

Matthew 24:21–22 (NKJV).

Jesus again states that the Saints go through the **Tribulation**—a unique period unlike any other in history with a determined endpoint, thus supporting a post-trib/pre-wrath rapture. He adds that unless the days of the **Great Tribulation** are shortened, *"no flesh would be saved."* On its surface, this passage seems to refer to the mortality of the Saints, but closer inspection of the original Greek also alludes to their eternal salvation. If their exposure time to Satan's unrestrained persecution is not curtailed, they risk "falling away" from their faith in despair by taking the mark of the Beast and participating in his one-world economic system. So, for *"the elect's sake"* and their eternal salvation, Jesus shortens their time on Earth by removing them from Satan's reach. Get ready for the **Day of Christ**—the *Rapture!*

CHAPTER 4

THE DAY OF CHRIST (RAPTURE)

At the end of the 7-year **Tribulation**, 3.5 Prophetic Years (1260 days) after the **Abomination of Desolation** in the **Third Temple,** Jesus appears on the heavenly clouds, gathers His believers in the air, and ascends back to Heaven with them.

The **Day of Christ** *is* the **Rapture** and should not be confused with the **Second Coming of Christ** (Apocalypse), also known as the Second Advent. That event occurs 2.9 Prophetic Years (1040 days) later when Jesus descends from Heaven with His armies to fight at the **Battle of Armageddon.**

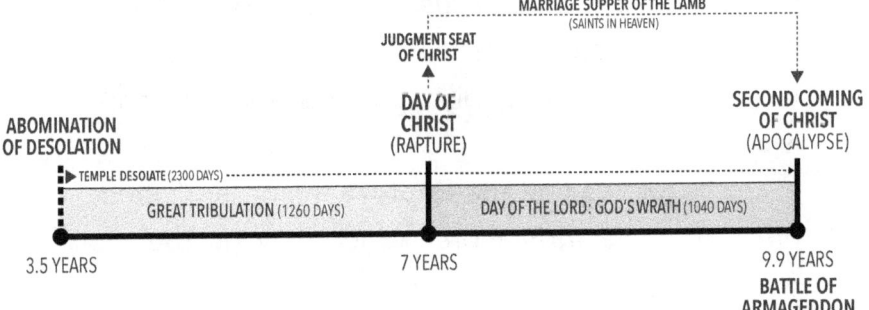

Here are some easy-to-remember differences between the **Day of Christ** (Rapture) and the **Second Coming of Christ** (Apocalypse):

DAY OF CHRIST (RAPTURE)	SECOND COMING OF CHRIST (APOCALYPSE)
Comes on the CLOUDS	Comes to the MOUNT OF OLIVES
Comes ALONE	Comes with His ARMIES
Comes FOR the Saints	Comes WITH the Saints
Brings REDEMPTION	Brings WRATH
Life for BELIEVERS	Death for UNBELIEVERS

There is also some understandable confusion between the terms *"Day of Christ"* and the *"Day of the Lord"* in Scripture. Both events initiate on the same day, so some verses may refer to one or the other, but the context often remains the same. There's also the fact that *"Christ is Lord,"* so some scriptures may innocently interchange or combine the two, such as the *"Day of the Lord Jesus."* And to top it off, many verses simply use the term, *"that day."* In most cases, the terms are correctly distinguished, and the context is clear.

Jesus tells us that the **Rapture** will occur *"immediately after the tribulation,"* which may be the most

4. The Day of Christ

concrete scriptural confirmation of a post-trib/pre-wrath rapture from Jesus Himself...

"**Immediately after the tribulation** of those days *[the 70th Week of Daniel]* **the sun will be darkened**, and the **moon will not give its light**; the **stars will fall from heaven**, and the powers of the heavens will be **shaken**. Then **the sign** *[image]* **of the Son of Man** *[Jesus]* **will appear in heaven** *[the sky]*, and then **all the tribes** *[nations]* **of the earth will mourn** *[unbelievers caught unprepared]*, and **they will see** the Son of Man coming **on the clouds of heaven** with power and great glory. And He will **send His angels** with a great **sound of a trumpet**, and **they will gather together His elect** *[the Saints]* **from the four winds** *[the furthest corners of the Earth]*, **from one end of heaven to the other.**" *[–Jesus]*

Matthew 24:29–31 (NKJV).

Jesus further describes a distinct celestial event that will precede His appearance: *"the sun will be darkened, and the moon will not give its light."* We can cross-reference this unique description with a verse from Joel, who describes this same celestial event occurring BEFORE the **Day of the Lord...**

---

*The **sun shall be turned into darkness**, And the **moon into blood**, **Before** the coming of the great and fantastic **day of the Lord**.*

Joel 2:31 (NKJV).

By describing the same celestial event that Jesus describes will precede His appearance immediately AFTER the **Tribulation,** Joel confirms here that the **Day of Christ** (Rapture) will occur BEFORE the **Day of the Lord,** supporting a post-trib/pre-wrath rapture.

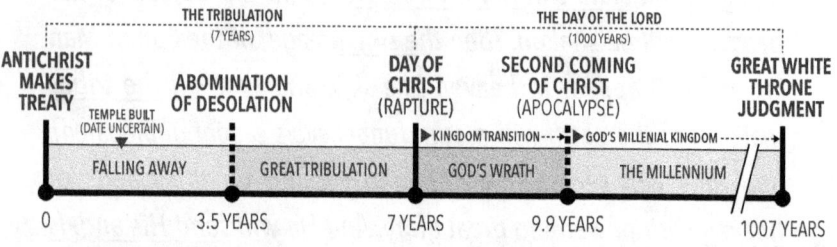

The **Day of Christ** (Rapture) is often referred to as *"the end"* in both the Old and New Testaments of the Bible, though this term has led to some confusion and debate. To clarify, this is *"the end"* of man's worldly empires—not the end of the Earth. It is the end of the **Great Tribulation** and the **Church Age.** The *"end of time"* and Earth as we know it occur 1000 years later, at the end of the **Day of the Lord: The Millennium.**

And he who overcomes, and <u>keeps My works until the end</u>, to him I will give <u>power over the nations</u> [in God's Millennial Kingdom]

Revelation 2:26 (NKJV).

Furthermore, *"the end"* of man's worldly empires means that **God's Millennial Kingdom** will replace them, because God does not allow the Earth to be without leadership. However, man's empires will not vanish overnight. The **Day of Christ** (Rapture) marks the beginning of a transition period that ultimately dissolves and replaces them, ending 2.9 Prophetic Years (1040 days) later at the **Second Coming of Christ** (Apocalypse).

A pre-trib rapture would not signify *"the end"* of man's worldly empires since they are allowed to expand and consolidate under the influence and authority of the Beast during the **Tribulation.** This presents another dilemma for the pre-trib rapture theory that we will explore further in the next section.

THE 6TH SEAL: THE RAPTURE

The **Day of Christ** (Rapture) begins when Jesus breaks the 6th seal of the 6th Holy Scroll in Heaven, initiating a series of prophetic events:
1. Cosmic disturbances
2. The voice of an archangel
3. The sign of Christ on the clouds
4. The dead Saints raised
5. The living Saints raptured
6. The Judgment Seat of Christ
7. The Marriage Supper of the Lamb

Breaking the 6th seal also marks the end of the **Great Tribulation** and the beginning of the **Day of**

the Lord (all on the same day). There's even more to explore in the next chapter, so let's unpack each of these events before we proceed.

COSMIC DISTURBANCES

After 6000 years, humanity's dominion over the world is set to be succeeded by Christ's reign for the next 1000 years in **God's Millennial Kingdom.** This is a momentous event that shakes the very foundations of Heaven and Earth...

And I beheld when he [Jesus] had <u>opened the sixth seal</u>, and, lo, there was a <u>great earthquake</u>; and the <u>sun became black</u> as sackcloth of hair, and the <u>moon became as blood</u> [deep red];

Revelation 6:12 (NKJV).

When Jesus breaks the 6th seal, it triggers a *"great earthquake."* This is the final earthquake of the **Tribulation,** so it's reasonable to assume that it is distinctly different from its predecessors. Coupling this *"great earthquake"* with astounding celestial events leaves no doubt that this is more than a mere coincidence.

As the verse continues, John describes a familiar celestial event in his vision: *"the sun became black"* and *"the moon became as blood."* Here, we again observe the same cosmic event that Jesus said would precede His appearance AFTER the **Tribulation** and which Joel stated would occur BEFORE the **Day of the Lord.** Linking these three verses from Jesus, Joel, and John, we see that the same celestial event will happen: 1) *"immediately after the tribulation,"* 2) *"before the Day of the Lord,"* and 3) when Jesus *"opened the sixth seal."* These truths confirm that the **Day of Christ** (Rapture) takes place immediately AFTER the **Tribulation** (the first 5 seals), AT the breaking of the 6th seal, and BEFORE the **Day of the Lord** (the 7th seal). This trifecta is a nuclear bomb against a pre-trib rapture theology. The passage continues…

And the stars of heaven fell to the earth, as a fig tree drops its late figs when it is shaken by a mighty wind.

Revelation 6:13 (NKJV).

The magnitude of this cosmic event is so extraordinary that it's difficult to fully comprehend. However, there are several theories about what these falling *"stars of heaven"* truly are. Since most stars we observe are fiery suns, and any nearby planetary impacts would undoubtedly annihilate the Earth, we must consider alternative explanations—the most plausible appearing to be meteorites or satellites. As of 2024, about 12,000 active satellites orbit the Earth, most of which belong to Starlink (starlink.com). By 2030, Starlink is projected to have 58,000 operational satellites. Add a few thousand defunct satellites and small meteorites, and that creates quite an aerial show, but the Earth remains intact.

A more intriguing theory suggests that these *"stars of heaven"* are angels descending from Heaven to Earth. The Bible repeatedly refers to angels as *"morning stars."* In the first scripture in this chapter, Jesus notes a further distinction...

"...the <u>stars will fall from heaven</u>, and the <u>powers of the heavens will be shaken</u>." [–Jesus]

Matthew 24:29 (NKJV)

"The powers of the heavens will be shaken" appears to extend beyond celestial bodies. This verse suggests a political upheaval within the *"powers"* of the Kingdom of Heaven itself. It's an extraordinary event and we have compelling passages from Revelation that align with it...

And another sign appeared in heaven: behold, a great, fiery red <u>dragon</u> [Satan] ... His tail drew <u>a third of the stars of heaven</u> and <u>threw them to the earth</u>.

Revelation 12:3–4 (NKJV)

4. The Day of Christ

It's unclear if these falling *"stars of heaven"* are visible to our eyes, but their description matches the cosmic disturbances that immediately precede the **Day of Christ** (Rapture). The passage continues…

And <u>war broke out in heaven</u>: Michael *[the archangel]* **and his angels fought with the dragon** *[Satan]***; and <u>the dragon and his angels fought, but they did not prevail</u>, nor was a place found for them in heaven <u>any longer</u>.**

Revelation 12:7–8 (NKJV).

So, Satan and his angels get their proverbial tails kicked and are permanently cast down to the terrestrial Earth—no longer permitted to transcend the heavens freely. The timing here is difficult to grasp, but consider that while Satan may have been censured long ago, many scriptures describe his comings and goings from Heaven to petition God, and this allowance may have extended to (at least some of) his angels—but not *"any longer"*…

So <u>the great dragon was cast out</u>, that serpent of old, called the <u>Devil and Satan</u>, who deceives the whole world; he was <u>cast to the earth</u>, and <u>his angels were cast out with him</u>. Then I heard a loud voice saying in heaven, "<u>Now salvation, and strength</u>, and the <u>kingdom of our God</u>, and the power of <u>His Christ have come</u>, *[to the Earth]* **for the <u>accuser</u>** *[Satan]* **of our <u>brethren</u>** *[the Saints]*,

<u>*who accused them before our God day and night*, has been <u>cast down</u></u> *[to the Earth].*

Revelation 12:9–10 (NKJV).

There it is. Satan has been accusing the Saints *"before our God day and night"* in Heaven, but that is no longer the case. His passport is officially revoked, and an angelic voice proclaims that Christ's reign is now established on Earth—an announcement decidedly linked to the 6th seal. This incredible sequence of events directly links Satan's permanent banishment from Heaven with the establishment of **God's Millennial Kingdom** (initiated by the 6th seal) and BEFORE **God's Wrath** is poured upon the world (initiated by the 7th seal). This is an essential point because, over the next 1040 days, the Beast's one-world government, the kings of the Earth, and their armies will be torn down under **God's Wrath** (Judgment), culminating in their final destruction at the **Battle of Armageddon.** Christ must reign over **God's Millennial Kingdom** WHILE the kingdoms of man are dismantled and replaced, lest there be a period without leadership on Earth…

For <u>He must reign</u> till He has put <u>all enemies</u> under His feet.

1 Corinthians 15:25 (NKJV).

4. The Day of Christ

A pre-trib rapture would not establish **God's Millennial Kingdom** on Earth, because we know that man's worldly empires would be allowed to GROW under the influence of the Beast during the **Tribulation.** The pre-tribulationist's attempt to merge the **Tribulation** with **God's Wrath** (Judgment) is paradoxical because the **Tribulation** is a time of unrestrained GROWTH for the Beast's one-world government, whereas **God's Wrath** signifies a period of tearing DOWN those worldly empires—both cannot occur simultaneously nor seamlessly without an additional bifurcation event. The only logical (and scriptural) resolution is a post-trib/pre-wrath rapture that ushers in Christ's reign AFTER the **Tribulation,** thus dismantling and replacing the Beast's one-world government empires with the establishment of **God's Millennial Kingdom** during the **Day of the Lord.**

The last cosmic disturbance is the hardest to imagine. The passage of Revelation 6 concludes...

Then the <u>sky receded as a scroll</u> when it is rolled up, and every <u>mountain and island</u> was <u>moved out of its place</u>.

Revelation 6:14 (NKJV).

The sky (or stars) receding *"as a scroll"* suggests that they vanish across a line or wave or seem to be pulled away. No further imagination is needed if this alludes to the banishment of Satan and his angels from the heavens. If God removes the sky and stars from our celestial view, that may be somewhat more complex, but we'll leave that to Him. If a more natural explanation is necessary, the sky and stars could be obscured by dust and ash from the earthquake(s) described in prior verses—possibly exacerbated by volcanic eruptions from *"every mountain and island"* being *"moved out of its place."*

Regardless of the ultimate explanation, the combination of these events sends a shockwave throughout humanity that heralds the end of man's empires and the onset of **God's Wrath** (Judgment)…

And the kings of the earth, the great men, the rich men, the commanders, the mighty men, every slave and every free man, <u>hid themselves</u> in the caves and in the rocks of the mountains, and said to the mountains and rocks, "Fall on us and <u>hide us from the face of Him</u> who sits on the throne [God] and from the wrath of the Lamb! [Jesus] For the <u>great day of His wrath</u> [Day of the Lord: God's Wrath] <u>has come</u>, and who is able to stand?"

Revelation 6:15–17 (NKJV).

They are correct; **God's Wrath** (Judgment) is coming soon. However, an extraordinary event must first occur for all the world to see.

THE VOICE OF AN ARCHANGEL

As if the preceding events haven't captured the world's full attention, the *"voice of an archangel,"* and the *"trumpet of God"* coming from the sky, serve as the audio cue for everyone on Earth to look up...

For the <u>Lord Himself</u> [Jesus] will descend from heaven with a <u>shout</u>, with the <u>voice of an archangel</u>, and with the <u>trumpet of God</u>. ...

---

1 Thessalonians 4:16 (NKJV).

The Greek word for *"archangel"* is *"archangelos"* and most accurately translates to the "chief" or "ruler" of angels. The only named archangel in the Bible is Michael, who is tasked with protecting the Jewish people. If there is more than one archangel in Heaven, it seems that Michael is the chief of them all.

The Bible does not describe the voice or the trumpet's sound, but it is reasonable to assume that they are overwhelming. These could be the earth-shattering sounds that awaken the *"dead in Christ,"* raising them from their graves of the past 2000 years.

THE SIGN OF CHRIST ON THE CLOUDS

At this point, the stage is set for the grandest entrance of all time, and the world gazes at the sky.

What they are about to see is unlike anything we have ever experienced...

Then <u>the sign of</u> the <u>Son of Man</u> [Jesus] will <u>appear in heaven</u>, and then <u>all the tribes of the earth</u> [nations] <u>will mourn</u> [being caught unprepared], and they will see the Son of Man coming <u>on the clouds of heaven</u> with power and great glory.

Luke 21:27 (NKJV).

This is the moment the Saints have prayed for over the past 2000 years. From this day forward, they will live eternally with Christ. The significance of this event far surpasses any attempt to describe it visually. Still, the scene raises a fundamental question: *"How does everyone on Earth see Jesus coming?"*

The assumption that Jesus appears as He left the Earth (as a man) may be limiting for this event. The verse adds, *"the sign of,"* which means not the thing itself or that by which a thing is recognized or distinguished. *"The sign of"* Jesus could be a cross, His likeness, or a spectacular representation of His glory. *"Appear in heaven"* and *"coming on the clouds of heaven"* suggest a more extraordinary celestial event, far above the clouds that affect our weather.

However Christ appears in the sky, the unsaved *"mourn"* because there is no mistaking who He is and why He has come. They are caught by surprise,

4. The Day of Christ

just as they were in the *"days of Noah,"* and they feel ashamed because they are unworthy to meet Him…

"But <u>as the days of Noah were</u>, so also will the <u>coming of the Son of Man be</u> [Day of Christ (Rapture)]. For as in the days before the flood, <u>they</u> [the unbelievers] were eating and drinking, marrying and giving in marriage, until the day that <u>Noah</u> [the Saints] entered the ark, and [the unbelievers] <u>did not know until the flood</u> [God's Wrath] came and <u>took them all away</u>, so also will the coming of the Son of Man be." [–Jesus]

Matthew 24:37–39 (NKJV).

The faithful Saints, however, are well-prepared to meet their Savior in the air BEFORE **God's Wrath** strikes the unbelievers left on Earth.

THE DEAD SAINTS RAISED

After Christ appears *"on the clouds of Heaven,"* He first raises the *"dead in Christ"*…

For the Lord Himself [Jesus] will descend from heaven with a shout, with the voice of an archangel, and with the trumpet of God. And the <u>dead in Christ</u> [deceased Saints] <u>will rise first</u>.

1 Thessalonians 4:16 (NKJV).

The *"dead in Christ"* are the Saints of the **Church Age**—all the believers who have died over the past

2000 years, from the time of Pentecost through the **Tribulation.** This group includes the martyred *"souls"* we learned about at the 5th seal—those who were put to death before and during the **Tribulation,** specifically for their faith in Christ. All the Saints of the **Church Age** have been *"resting"* in Heaven for this day.

The souls of the deceased Saints are brought down from Heaven to be resurrected into their new, glorified spiritual bodies, formed from the dust and ashes of their earthly bodies. This process accounts for bodies that have decomposed, been cremated, been lost at sea, and so forth. This event is the SECOND PART of the FIRST RESURRECTION. (See Chapter 6: The First & Second Resurrections.)

So also is the <u>resurrection of the dead</u>. The [natural] body is sown in corruption, it is <u>raised in incorruption</u>. It is sown in dishonor, it is <u>raised in glory</u>. It is sown in weakness, it is <u>raised in power</u>. It is sown a natural body, it is <u>raised a spiritual body</u>. There is a natural body, and there is a [glorified] <u>spiritual body</u>.

1 Corinthians 15:42–44 (NKJV).

Unlike their natural (mortal) bodies, their glorified spiritual (immortal) bodies are powerful, incorruptible, and imperishable—immune to extreme temperatures, sickness, hunger, and thirst. However, they can enjoy

4. The Day of Christ

banquets and wine in Heaven if they choose. They possess a physical form and reside in a physical world. The Saints of all times (past and future) experience this same physical transformation, and they are all part of the FIRST RESURRECTION.

THE LIVING SAINTS RAPTURED

Immediately after the *"dead in Christ"* are raised into the heavenly clouds with Jesus, the living Saints are gathered to meet them in the air. This is the **Rapture.**

Then we [the Saints] <u>**who are alive and remain**</u> *shall be* <u>**caught up together with them**</u> *[the dead in Christ]* <u>**in the clouds**</u> *to meet the Lord [Jesus]* <u>**in the air.**</u> *And thus we shall* <u>**always be with the Lord.**</u>

---

1 Thessalonians 4:17 (NKJV).

The raptured Saints of the **Tribulation** also require their spiritual bodies to prepare for their ascent through the atmosphere, other dimensions, and ultimately to Heaven. Their physical transformation occurs shortly after they are lifted from the Earth's surface and before reaching their brethren *"in the clouds."* This is "the **Rapture** of the Church" and is included in the SECOND PART of the FIRST RESURRECTION. These raptured Saints avoid a mortal death. (See Chapter 6: The First & Second Resurrections.)

> *Behold, I tell you a mystery: <u>We shall not all sleep</u> [die a mortal death], but <u>we shall all be changed</u> [transformed] in a moment, in the twinkling of an eye, at the last <u>trumpet</u> [on the Day of Christ]. For the trumpet will sound, and <u>the dead will be raised</u> [first] incorruptible, and <u>we shall be changed</u> [into our spiritual bodies].*
>
> 1 Corinthians 15:50–52 (NKJV).

The **Rapture** at the end of the **Great Tribulation** spares the **Tribulation** Saints from the next 1040 days (2.9 Prophetic Years), during which **God's Wrath** (Judgment) is unleashed upon the world. At this point, our timeline splits to account for simultaneous events in the heavens and on Earth. The remainder of this chapter focuses on the heavenly events.

THE JUDGMENT SEAT OF CHRIST

Once all the Saints of the **Church Age** are gathered in the air, they are taken to Heaven (or perhaps to one of the "heavenly places") and assembled at the **Judgment Seat of Christ**...

> *...I looked, and behold, a <u>great multitude</u> which <u>no one could number</u>, of <u>all nations, tribes, peoples, and tongues</u>, standing before the throne and <u>before the Lamb</u>, [the Judgment Seat of Christ] <u>clothed with white robes</u>, ...*
>
> Revelation 7:9 (NKJV).

The number of Saints accumulated in 2000 years is beyond reasonable counting. Comprising people *"of all nations, tribes, peoples, and tongues,"* they serve as the ultimate example of diversity on Earth, united by their shared belief in Christ.

---

*...So he [the angel] **said to me, "These are the ones** [the Saints] **who come out of the great tribulation, and washed their robes and made them white in the blood of the Lamb** [Jesus]. ..."*

Revelation 7:14 (NKJV).

The angel in this verse emphasizes the Saints *"who come out of the great tribulation"*—those who were martyred (as seen at the 5th seal) or lived to be **Raptured** (at the 6th seal)—clearly illustrating a post-trib rapture. All the Saints of the **Church Age** stand before Jesus at the **Judgment Seat of Christ** to receive rewards based on their works—or lack thereof. The **Tribulation** Saints are assured special rewards, as we will soon see.

---

*For we [Saints of the Church Age] **must all appear before the judgment seat of Christ**, that **each one may receive** [judgment for] the things done in the body, **according to what** [works] **he has done**, whether **good or bad**.*

---

2 Corinthians 5:10 (NKJV).

It's important to note that works in life have nothing to do with eternal salvation (or damnation). This judgment event should not be confused with the final **Great White Throne Judgment,** which occurs 1000 years later, at the end of the **Millennium**—that event is for everyone! The **Judgment Seat of Christ** is only for the Saints of the **Church Age** gathered at the end of the **Great Tribulation.** Their presence here signifies that they have already accepted Christ as their savior and secured eternal salvation through their faith and God's grace—not their works...

For <u>**by grace you have been saved through faith**</u> *[in Christ],* ***and that*** <u>***not of yourselves;***</u> ***it is the*** <u>***gift of God,***</u> ***not of works,*** ***lest anyone should boast*** *[that they earned it].*

Ephesians 1:8–9

So, setting eternal salvation aside, what is the reward for their faithful works in life—or lack thereof—as followers and witnesses of Christ's teachings? If they are found lacking in their faithful works and preparedness, we can only presume they exit through a side door and go directly to Heaven. If they are found worthy in their faithful works and preparedness, we can imagine they proceed through a grand victory arch to be rewarded with future roles of authority in Heaven and **God's Millennial Kingdom** on Earth (under Christ's reign). However, before that, their first reward is an exclusive invitation to attend…

THE MARRIAGE SUPPER OF THE LAMB

This grand celebration in Heaven unites the Church as the Bride of Christ with the Bridegroom, Jesus, signifying the final phase of a traditional Jewish wedding custom.

Then he said to me, "Write: **'Blessed are those who are called** *[selected to attend]* **to the marriage supper of the Lamb!'**

Revelation 19:9 (NKJV).

The first phase, the betrothal period—what we refer to as the engagement—was completed when the Saints put their faith in Christ as their Savior, and the bridegroom's parent (God the Father) paid the dowry with the blood of Christ, shed on the Bride's behalf. The second phase is fulfilled with the **Rapture** of the Church—when the bridegroom claims His bride and leads her to his house (or his Father's house) in a procession along with his companions and her maidens. The wedding feast signifies the consummation of the marriage.

This event's scale, majesty, and joy exceed our imagination. The most lavish celebrations in Earth's history pale in comparison, and this time, it is not limited to the wealthy, world leaders, or royalty. Faithful works for God's Kingdom merit this reward, and the martyred and **Tribulation** Saints receive exclusive honor…

"And everyone who has left houses or brothers or sisters or father or mother or wife or children or lands, <u>for My name's sake</u>, shall <u>receive a hundredfold</u>, and <u>inherit eternal life</u>." [–Jesus]

Matthew 19:29 (NKJV).

The **Marriage Supper of the Lamb** lasts 1040 days (2.9 Prophetic Years including the **Judgment Seat of Christ**) while **God's Wrath** (Judgment) is poured out on the Earth. The Lord has removed the Saints BEFORE the time of His wrath and holds them safely in Heaven until His judgment of *"those who dwell on the earth"* is complete.

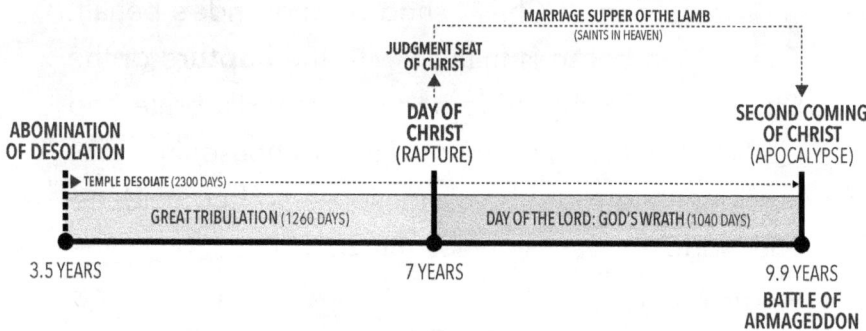

CHAPTER 5
THE DAY OF THE LORD: GOD'S WRATH

The **Day of the Lord** is the 1000-year period immediately following the **Day of Christ** (Rapture) at the end of the **Great Tribulation,** beginning on the same day. It signifies *"the end"* of man's worldly empires and ushers in **God's Millennial Kingdom** on Earth under Christ's reign.

There are two components of these 1000 years:

1. **God's Wrath:** the initial 2.9 years (1040 days) leading up to the **Second Coming of Christ** (Apocalypse) and the **Battle of Armageddon** (this chapter).

2. **The Millennium:** the 997.1 years of peace during which Jesus rules the world's nations *"with a rod of iron,"* culminating in **Satan's Final Rebellion** and the **Great White Throne Judgment** (the next chapter).

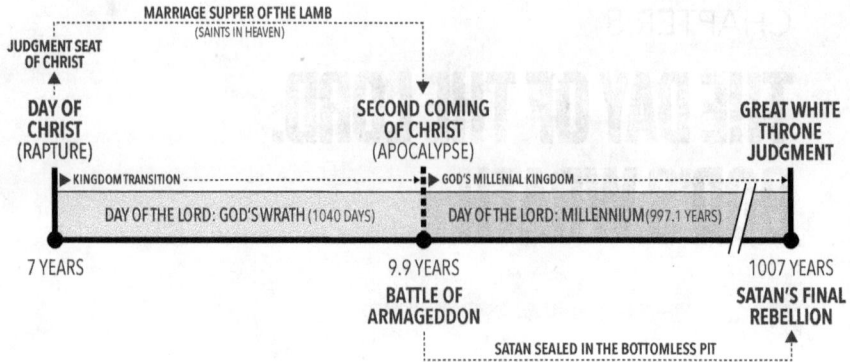

Immediately after the **Rapture,** four angels *"stand at the four corners of the earth"* to soothe the weather by restraining the *"four winds,"* resulting in a calm and eerie silence...

<u>*After these things*</u> [*the events of the 6th seal*] <u>*I saw four angels standing at the four corners*</u> *of the earth,* <u>*holding the four winds*</u> *of the earth, that* <u>*the wind should not blow*</u> *on the earth, on the sea, or on any tree.*

Revelation 7:1 (NKJV).

Not a leaf or stalk trembles and the sea is as smooth as glass. This atmospheric silence is created in reverence for the opening of the 7th seal, initiating **God's Wrath** (Judgment) upon the Earth. This is truly the calm before the storm. But first, God must seal His 144,000 servants.

THE 144,000 OF ISRAEL SEALED

Moments after the **Rapture** of the Church, God's **Two Witnesses,** carried over from the **Great Tribulation,** are the only Saints left on Earth to spread the gospel of Christ. These two prophets have been active for much of their 42-month assignment, preaching and performing miracles in Jerusalem, experiencing varying levels of success and disdain. Among their followers are 144,000 young Jews, representing 12,000 from each of the 12 tribes of Israel. The 144,000 could be a literal number, though 12,000 x 12 might also symbolize completeness and represent all Jews. After witnessing the **Rapture** of the Church, these "144,000" Jews repent by accepting Christ as their true Messiah and savior…

"And I will pour on the <u>house of David</u> [Israel] and on the <u>inhabitants of Jerusalem</u> [the Jews] the Spirit of <u>grace</u> [forgiveness] and <u>supplication</u> [answer to prayer]; then they will <u>look on Me</u> [the Lord] <u>whom they pierced</u> [on the cross]. Yes, they will <u>mourn for Him</u> [Jesus] as one mourns for <u>his only son</u>, and grieve for Him as one grieves for a <u>firstborn</u>."

Zechariah 12:10 (NKJV).

God's chosen people are redeemed after 2000 years *"in the wilderness."* These 144,000 (possibly all Jews) are appointed as special *"servants of God"* to continue spreading the gospel of Christ for the next 1040 days while **God's Wrath** (Judgment) is poured upon the Earth. God places His Holy Seal (a signet of ownership) on their foreheads to protect them from His wrath during this time of judgment...

..."*Do not harm the earth, the sea, or the trees till we have <u>sealed the servants of our God</u> on their foreheads.*" *And I heard the number of those who were sealed. One hundred and forty-four thousand [144,000] of <u>all the tribes</u> of the <u>children of Israel</u> were <u>sealed</u>:*"

Revelation 7:3–4 (NKJV).

This sealing of the 144,000 is pinpointed AFTER the end of the **Tribulation** and the **Rapture** (both events of the first 6 seals) and BEFORE the 7th seal ushers in the 7 trumpets and 7 bowls of **God's Wrath.** This distinct bifurcation differentiates the **Tribulation** from the **Day of the Lord,** further supporting a post-trib/pre-wrath rapture.

These "*servants of God:*" 1) preach the Gospel of Christ during the devastations of **God's Wrath** (Judgment), 2) witness the **Second Coming of Christ** (Apocalypse), 3) join Jesus and His army at the **Battle of Armageddon,** and 4) live well into the **Millennium** to see the restoration of Jerusalem and their **Temple.** Given the longevity promised during the **Millennium** (as we'll see later), they could: 5) live long enough to fight against **Satan's Final Rebellion** at the end of the **Millennium,** and 6) be raptured in the THIRD PART of the FIRST RESURRECTION. (See Chapter 6: The First & Second Resurrections.)

THE 7TH SEAL: SILENCE IN HEAVEN

When Jesus breaks the seal of the 7th Holy Scroll, a brief silence falls over the *"great multitude"* before the throne of God in Heaven...

When He [Jesus] opened the seventh seal, there was <u>silence in heaven</u> for about half an hour.

Revelation 8:1 (NKJV).

This silent interlude replaces the ongoing praises at the throne of God—an appropriate reflection of the Lord's impending judgment. It also creates a pause to secure the sealing of the 144,000 Jews.

And I saw the <u>seven angels</u> who stand before God, and to them were given <u>seven trumpets</u>.

Revelation 8:2 (NKJV).

This is the 7th (and final) Holy Scroll, and breaking its protective seal unleashes a sevenfold series of judgments, each initiated by an angel's trumpet. The

Day of the Lord has begun, and **God's Wrath** (Judgment) is about to be poured upon the Earth...

Then the angel took the <u>censer</u> [golden bowl], <u>filled it with fire</u> from the altar [of God], and <u>threw it to the earth</u>. And there were <u>noises, thunderings, lightnings,</u> and an <u>earthquake</u>.

Revelation 8:5 (NKJV).

God's Wrath (Judgment) is the most troubling and graphic stage of the end times, and the details are difficult to imagine. The good news for the Saints is that they are NOT present during this period. They were removed during the **Rapture** earlier in the day, are on their way to the **Judgment Seat of Christ,** and many of them will attend the **Marriage Supper of the Lamb** until the last of **God's Wrath** (Judgment) is poured upon the Earth.

The good news for the unsaved who must endure this period is that, by God's grace, they still have time to repent and accept Christ as their Lord and Savior. Many souls are saved during this time, and many pay for their faith with their lives, as did many Saints during the **Tribulation.** The bad news for the Beast, the kings of the Earth, and their armies is that they will be among the hardest hit when these judgments are unleashed upon the Earth, and their days are now precisely numbered at 1040.

THE 7 TRUMPET JUDGMENTS

So the seven angels who had the seven trumpets [of Judgment] prepared themselves to sound.

Revelation 8:6 (NKJV).

Many of the afflictions about to be initiated by the angel's trumpets seem quite literal. However, some may allude to God using man's aggression to carry out His will, such as military operations between nations. **God's Wrath** (Judgment) on the world at this time is just and deserved. Still, His primary purpose is to "shake the tree" by awakening people to repent and bringing as many as possible into His Kingdom. During the **Tribulation,** God used His faithful Saints to witness and offer prayers of salvation to the unbelievers. As the unsaved enter the **Day of the Lord,** they will have the **Two Witnesses** (for a few months) and the 144,000 Jews to teach the Gospel of Christ and offer repentance to as many as will receive Him.

Readers of the Old Testament will recognize that God's impending judgments reflect many of the plagues He inflicted on Egypt to compel Pharaoh to free the Israelites from slavery. These similarities are not coincidental. God often utilizes patterns in prophecy, and this mechanism is especially important for Jewish interpretations of Scripture.

The first 4 angels' trumpets unleash a series of sequential devastations upon the Earth, sea, waters, and sky; however, with each, the damage is limited to *"a third."* This limitation illustrates God's restraint in allowing more time for the unsaved to repent while simultaneously predicting total devastation for those who ignore His warnings and choose to oppose Him.

THE 1ST TRUMPET: VEGETATION STRUCK

The first angel sounded [his trumpet]: And <u>hail and fire</u> followed, <u>mingled with blood</u>, and they were thrown to the earth. And a <u>third of the trees</u> were burned up, and <u>all green grass</u> was burned up.

Revelation 8:7 (NKJV).

The combination of *"hail and fire"* may seem contradictory, but many possibilities exist, including lightning strikes, meteoric or volcanic activity, or a symbolic reference to devastation. Regardless of its exact form, the target is one-third of all plant life and *"all green grass."* The phrase *"mingled with blood"* may refer to injuries sustained by people and livestock, as well as famine resulting from the loss of food crops, grazing lands, and herds. This event resembles the 7th plague in Egypt when God sent thunder, hail, and fire over the land.

THE 2ND TRUMPET: SEAS STRUCK

Then the second angel sounded [his trumpet]: **And something like a <u>great mountain burning with fire</u> was <u>thrown into the sea</u>, and a <u>third of the sea</u> became blood. And a <u>third of the living creatures in the sea died</u>, and a <u>third of the ships were destroyed</u>.**

Revelation 8:8–9 (NKJV).

The imagery suggests a major catastrophe, such as a large meteorite strike or a volcanic eruption, potentially occurring in the Mediterranean Sea—a region with significant underwater volcanic activity. Both of these disasters could yield similar consequences. Direct impacts could obliterate ships, while the wider effects of tidal waves and surges would likely cause more vessels in port to break apart. Again, the damage is confined to *"a third."*

THE 3RD TRUMPET: FRESH WATERS STRUCK

Then the third angel sounded [his trumpet]: **And <u>a great star</u> fell from heaven, <u>burning like a torch</u>, and it fell on a <u>third of the rivers</u> and on the <u>springs of water</u>. The name of the star is Wormwood. A <u>third of the waters became wormwood</u>, and many men <u>died from the water</u>, because it was made bitter.**

Revelation 8:10–11 (NKJV).

"Wormwood" is mentioned eight times in the Old Testament to describe bitterness, poison, and death, suggesting that naming the star here may reflect its effects rather than serving as a proper noun. While the 2nd angel's trumpet affects a third of the sea, this event embitters a third of the Earth's fresh (drinking) water, leading to mass poisoning and death.

Similar to the previous catastrophe, the imagery appears to describe a large meteorite. Another possibility could be a nuclear missile *"burning like a torch"* and contaminating the drinking and ground waters with radioactive fallout. Other interpretations suggest an angel falling from Heaven like a burning star, which we find in the 5th trumpet verse and other scriptures.

These events of the 2nd and 3rd trumpets are reminiscent of the first plague on Egypt when God turned the Nile River into "blood," killing all the fish and rendering the water unusable and undrinkable.

THE 4TH TRUMPET: HEAVENS STRUCK

Then the fourth angel sounded [his trumpet]: ***And a <u>third of the sun</u> was struck, a <u>third of the moon</u>, and a <u>third of the stars</u>, so that a third of them were darkened. A third of the day did not shine, and likewise the night.***

Revelation 8:12 (NKJV).

5. God's Wrath

This event resembles the 9th plague on Egypt, which brought a *"darkness which may even be felt"* over the land for three days. It is also similar to the last verse from the opening of the 6th seal, *"Then the sky receded as a scroll..."* In this case, a third of the light is removed from both the day and night.

The logical cause of this increased darkness could be smoke and ash from burning forests and cities, obscuring the sun, moon, and stars. An equally plausible explanation (though harder to imagine) is that God obscures them on a celestial level. The darkness may also serve as reverence for the three escalating judgments about to unfold, similar to the cosmic disturbances that preceded the breaking of the 6th seal before the **Rapture.**

And I looked, and I heard an angel flying through the midst of heaven, saying with a loud voice, "Woe, woe, woe to the inhabitants of the earth, because of the <u>remaining blasts</u> of the trumpet of the three angels <u>who are about to sound!</u>"

Revelation 8:13 (NKJV).

THE 5TH TRUMPET: LOCUST ARMY

Then the fifth angel sounded [his trumpet]: **And I saw a <u>star</u>** *[angel]* **<u>fallen from heaven to the earth</u>. To him was given <u>the key to the bottomless pit</u>** *[the Abyss of Hades].* **And he opened the bot-**

tomless pit, and smoke arose out of the pit like the smoke of a great furnace. So the <u>sun and the air were darkened</u> because of the smoke of the pit.

Revelation 9:1–2 (NKJV).

The opening verse echoes Jesus' words in the book of Luke: *"I saw Satan fall like lightning from heaven."* Satan and his fallen angels were permanently banished from Heaven during the events of the 6th seal, so this is a servant angel of God, as we will see in a similar occurrence later. God gives His angel the key and permission to *"open the bottomless pit."* Other translations refer to it as *"the shaft of the Abyss"* and these names speak for themselves. Unlocking the pit releases such a vast amount of smoke that it darkens the sun and sky, likely contributing to the darkening effect of the previous angel's trumpet. The plagues affect all but the 144,000 Jews sealed with God's protection…

Then out of the smoke <u>locusts came upon the earth</u>. And to them <u>was given power</u>, as the <u>scorpions</u> of the earth have power. They were commanded <u>not to harm the grass</u> of the earth, <u>or any green thing, or any tree</u>, but <u>only those men who do not have the seal of God</u> on their foreheads [all but the 144,000 Jews].

Revelation 9:3–4 (NKJV).

5. God's Wrath

This event resembles the 8th plague on Egypt when God unleashed a dreadful infestation of locusts that covered the land. In contrast, those locusts were insects that consumed all the vegetation, as locusts do. These *"locusts"* are compared to insects, but are part of Satan's army and possess the ability to sting fiercely and repeatedly. Their mandate is to disregard vegetation and explicitly to torment humanity for 5 months—but not kill them...

And they were <u>not given authority to kill them</u> [*those without God's seal*], ***but to <u>torment them for five months.</u> Their torment was like the torment of a <u>scorpion</u> when it strikes a man. In those days men will seek death and will not find it; they will desire to die, and <u>death will flee from them.</u>***

Revelation 9:5–6 (NKJV).

Their affliction is so intense that *"men will seek death"* rather than continue to suffer, but *"death will flee from them."* Similar to the story of Job (which we discussed in Chapter 2), God permits Satan to torment but not to kill at this time. Furthermore, God has limited humanity's torment here to 5 months.

These *"locusts"* are depicted (in symbolic detail) as horses ready for battle, adorned with crowns, featuring human faces, women's hair, lion's teeth, iron breastplates, loud wings, and tails resembling scorpions. Numerous theories exist, including military forces like helicopters, drones, or tactical robots. Another possibility is demonic spirits controlling dreadful beasts, with a strong likelihood of hybrid biotech and artificial intelligence.

And they [the locust beasts] **had as king over them** *the angel of the bottomless pit, whose name in Hebrew is* **Abaddon**, *but in Greek he has the name* **Apollyon**.

Revelation 9:11 (NKJV).

These beasts have a commander, emphasizing the idea of a military structure. The literal translation of Abaddon/Apollyon is "one who destroys." This name is often associated with Satan, but in this verse, it likely refers to one of his underlings—or potentially a military leader or ruler.

THE 6TH TRUMPET: EUPHRATES ANGELS RELEASED

*Then the sixth angel sounded [his trumpet]: And I heard a voice from the four horns [corners] of the golden altar which is before God, saying to the sixth angel who had the trumpet, "***Release the four angels who are bound at the great river Euphrates***." So the four angels,* **who had been prepared** *for the* **hour and day and month and year**, *were released to* **kill a third of mankind**.

Revelation 9:13–15 (NKJV).

5. God's Wrath

These four angels, bound at (or below) the Euphrates River, are so mighty and terrible that they have been chained and imprisoned until their appointed *"hour and day and month and year."* Interestingly, the Euphrates River, the most extensive river system in Western Asia, has been drying up at an alarming rate since 2003, revealing several ancient ruins and previously submerged man-made caves. Online videos claim to have recorded supernatural voices, screams, and rattling chains echoing from deep within these recently exposed caves. These videos are convincing and easy to find online.

Now the number of the <u>army of the horsemen</u> was <u>two hundred million</u> [200,000,000]; I heard the number of them. And thus I saw the <u>horses</u> in the vision: those who sat on them had <u>breastplates</u> of fiery red, hyacinth blue, and sulfur yellow; and the heads of the horses were like the <u>heads of lions</u>; and out of their mouths came fire, smoke, and brimstone. [...] For their <u>power is in their mouth and in their tails</u>; for their tails are like serpents, having heads; and with them they do harm.

Revelation 9:16–17, 19 (NKJV).

This cavalry mirrors the swarm of locusts from the previous angel's trumpet, featuring lion's teeth whose *"power is in their mouths and tails"* and whose riders don breastplates. Again, we're likely observing strong symbolic imagery here, suggesting a well-organized army of demons, beasts, or military forces. The astonishing number of 200 million signifies an army unlike any known today; thus, perhaps these are joint forces composed of the natural and spiritual realms.

Whatever this army comprises, they seem to follow the four fallen angels into battle, and the Beast is their ultimate commander. They unleash unprecedented bloodshed and suffering, but God restrains them to the point of *"killing a third of mankind."* Considering the impact of the prior events up to this point, the number killed here could reach 2 billion people.

This is the last restrained judgment warning from God, and the next sevenfold series will be complete. By this time, hundreds of millions have repented and secured eternal salvation before their death. For those who have survived thus far, their time to repent is running short; however, instead of repenting for their transgressions, they remain loyal to the Beast and continue to revel in their mortal sins...

But the rest of mankind, who were <u>not killed by these plagues</u>, <u>did not repent</u> of the works of their hands, ... And <u>they did not repent</u> of their murders or their sorceries or their sexual immorality or their thefts.

Revelation 9:20–21 (NKJV).

THE TWO WITNESSES KILLED & RESURRECTED

When they [the Two Witnesses] finish their testimony, <u>the beast</u> [Satan] that ascends out of the bottomless pit will make war against them, overcome them, and <u>kill them</u>.

Revelation 11:7 (NKJV).

After 1260 days (3.5 Prophetic Years) since their appearance, the **Two Witnesses** have been unstoppable. They have summoned fire from Heaven and struck the world's inhabitants with plagues, all while prophesying the return of the Lord and emphasizing the urgency to repent. They have fulfilled their mission, and God removes His protection over them. The Beast moves in quickly, destroys their ministry, kills them, and makes a spectacle of their bodies...

Then those from the <u>peoples, tribes, tongues, and nations</u> will <u>see their dead bodies</u> three-and-a-half [3.5] days, and not allow their dead bodies to be put into graves. And those who dwell on the earth <u>will rejoice over them,</u> <u>make merry,</u> and <u>send gifts to one another,</u> because these two prophets tormented <u>those who dwell on the earth</u> [the unsaved].

Revelation 11:9–10 (NKJV).

Their corpses are left in the street for 3.5 days for all the world to see. This desecration of their bodies represents a victory for the Beast and provides great satisfaction to the unsaved whom they offended and tormented. Some rejoice at their deaths, attend celebrations, and even exchange gifts. This verse is seen as remarkably prophetic of our current era. When it was written, the notion of the entire world gazing upon a single event was inconceivable. Today, live-streaming videos from our smartphones to millions of global viewers is commonplace.

Now <u>after</u> the three-and-a-half [3.5] days the <u>breath of life from God entered them</u>, and <u>they stood on their feet</u>, and <u>great fear fell on those</u> [unsaved] who saw them. And they <u>heard a loud voice from heaven</u> saying to them, "Come up here." And <u>they ascended to heaven</u> in a cloud, and <u>their enemies saw them</u>.

Revelation 11:11–12 (NKJV).

The reveling unsaved of the world feel their blood run ice cold when they see the dead bodies of the **Two Witnesses** resurrect and rise to their feet. Shock, terror, and dread are mere understatements when they hear the Lord's voice say, *"Come up here,"* and watch as the **Two Witnesses** are raptured *"to heaven in a cloud."*

In the same hour there was a <u>great earthquake</u> [in Jerusalem], and a <u>tenth of the city fell</u>. In the earthquake <u>seven thousand</u>

5. God's Wrath

[7,000] <u>people were killed</u>, and the rest were afraid and <u>gave glory to the God of heaven</u>.

Revelation 11:13 (NKJV).

God's judgment promptly falls upon the Gentile (non-Jewish) trespassers in Jerusalem for their mistreatment of His **Two Witnesses,** manifesting as a *"great earthquake"* that claims the lives of 7,000 people. This event brings to mind the earthquake that struck Jerusalem when Jesus died on the cross at Calvary, but it is far more severe. The survivors respond with fear and reverence to God's power, but it's unclear how many repent.

THE 7TH TRUMPET: GOD'S KINGDOM PROCLAIMED

Then the seventh angel sounded [his trumpet]: **And there were loud voices in heaven, saying, "The <u>kingdoms of this world</u>** *[ruled by men]* **have <u>become the kingdoms of our Lord</u> and of His Christ, and <u>He shall reign forever and ever!</u>"**

Revelation 11:15 (NKJV).

This is the 7th (and final) trumpet blast from the angels standing before God's throne. Similar to the 7th (and final) seal, the 7th angel's trumpet provides an interlude before the next series of judgments: the 7 Bowls of Wrath. However, instead of reverent silence, loud voices and spontaneous worship erupt, proclaiming the end of man's *"kingdoms of this world"* and the beginning of Christ's eternal reign on Earth. The next verse offers a glimpse into the heart of Heaven. The temple of God is opened, and the *"ark of His covenant"* is unveiled...

Then <u>the temple of God was opened in heaven</u>, and the <u>ark of His covenant</u> was seen in His temple. And there were <u>lightnings, noises, thunderings</u>, an <u>earthquake</u>, and <u>great hail</u>.

Revelation 11:19 (NKJV).

This is likely not the same Ark lost to history around 2600 years ago and popularized in the first Indiana Jones movie. God instructed Moses to oversee the construction of that Ark on Earth, following precise measurements and materials, presumably to match an original Ark in Heaven. Whether the Ark in this heavenly vision is the original or a symbol, it likely represents God's presence and preservation for His people (the Jews). Seeing it here may also suggest that the Earthly Ark will soon be discovered and revealed to the world. The 7th angel's trumpet has sounded, and the final sevenfold series of judgments—the 7 Bowls of Wrath—are about to be poured upon the Earth.

5. God's Wrath

THE FINAL WARNING

A trio of angels proclaim God's final warning to the remaining inhabitants of Earth before the final series of judgments. For those still aligning with the Beast and participating in his economic system—even as a means of survival—their time to repent for their transgressions against God and attain their eternal salvation is running out. The 1st angel declares the "everlasting gospel" to the world…

Then I saw another angel flying in the midst of heaven, having the <u>everlasting gospel</u> to preach <u>to those who dwell on the earth</u> –to every nation, tribe, tongue, and people–saying with a loud voice, "<u>Fear God and give glory to Him</u>, for the <u>hour of His judgment has come</u> [time is almost up]; and <u>worship Him</u> who made heaven and earth, the sea and springs of water."

Revelation 14:6–7 (NKJV). .

Some repent in the final series of judgments but must still endure them. Should they die, they will be blessed and receive rewards in Heaven to compensate for their suffering. Not a bad deal…

Then I heard a voice from heaven saying to me, "Write: '<u>Blessed are the dead who die</u> [believing] <u>in the Lord from now on</u>.' "…

Revelation 14:13 (NKJV).

The other 2 angels pronounce God's final series of judgments on the kingdoms of the Beast and his worshipers. By this time, there is no question about God's authority, justice, or His countless offers for the unsaved rebellion to repent, but the darkness of the Beast has made their hearts like clay, and God's light only hardens them more. With this final warning, any excuses are removed for all who will stand before the Lord at the **Great White Throne Judgment.**

THE 7 BOWLS OF WRATH

Then I saw another sign in heaven, great and marvelous: <u>seven angels</u> having the <u>seven last plagues</u>, for in them the <u>wrath of God is complete</u>.

Revelation 15:1 (NKJV).

These 7 angels execute 7 plagues that conclude the outpouring of God's judgments upon a world that has rejected Him and aligned with the Beast. Each angel is entrusted with a *"golden bowl full of the wrath of God"*...

Then one of the four living creatures [at the throne of God] **gave to the seven angels <u>seven golden bowls full of the wrath of God</u> who lives forever and ever.**

Revelation 15:7 (NKJV).

5. God's Wrath

Only God has the authority to administer judgment, so He commands the 7 angels to pour their bowls onto the Earth...

Then I heard a loud voice from the temple [God] saying to the seven angels, "Go and pour out <u>the bowls of the wrath of God</u> on the earth."

Revelation 16:1 (NKJV).

The first 4 angels' bowls release plagues that parallel the devastations of the first 4 angel's trumpets: Earth, sea, waters, and sky. This time, however, their effect is not limited to *"a third"*—their destruction is total. It seems that the judgments poured from each bowl expand upon the judgments released by each trumpet.

THE 1ST BOWL: LOATHSOME SORE

So the first [angel] went and poured out his bowl <u>upon the earth</u>, and <u>a foul and loathsome sore</u> came upon the men <u>who had the mark of the beast</u> and those <u>who worshiped his image</u> [idol].

Revelation 16:2 (NKJV).

While the 1st angel's trumpet devastated the surface of the Earth, the 1st angel's bowl affects Earth's inhabitants—specifically, those who worshiped the Beast. *"A foul and loathsome sore"* comes upon those "who had the mark of the beast," presumably at the location of their mark! This plague resembles the 6th plague on Egypt when God caused boils and sores to break out on the bodies of the Egyptians.

THE 2ND BOWL: SEA TO BLOOD

Then the second angel poured out his bowl <u>on the sea</u>, and it became <u>blood as of a dead man</u>; and <u>every living creature in the sea died</u>.

Revelation 16:3 (NKJV)

Similar to the 2nd angel's trumpet, the 2nd angel's bowl impacts the sea and its creatures; however, this time, the destruction is complete, leading to the death of all marine life. The phrase *"blood as of a dead man"* suggests an analogy to putrefying fluids, akin to those of a corpse—not a literal transformation of water into blood. It is unclear whether this damage extends to the depths of the world's oceans, but the devastation of the seas in the Middle East is absolute.

THE 3RD BOWL: FRESH WATERS TO BLOOD

Then the third angel poured out his bowl <u>on the rivers and springs</u> of water, and <u>they became blood</u>.

Revelation 16:4 (NKJV)

Like the 3rd angel's trumpet, the 3rd angel's bowl pollutes the fresh waters, which are crucial for drinking, animals, and agriculture. The Earth is now headed toward planetary extinction. This plague resembles the 1st plague on Egypt when God turned the Nile River into *"blood,"* killing all the fish and rendering the water undrinkable.

THE 4TH BOWL: SCORCHING SUN

Then the fourth angel poured out his bowl <u>on the sun</u>, and power was given to him to <u>scorch men with fire</u>.

Revelation 16:8 (NKJV).

While the 4th angel's trumpet darkened the sun, the 4th angel's bowl intensifies the sun's power. Temperatures on Earth rise to such extremes that the heat scorches flesh. Since the angel pours the bowl's contents *"on the sun,"* this could indicate increased solar activity and flares. The extreme heating effect could also be a result of the removal of Earth's atmospheric defenses that restrain the sun's potency and radiation. The lack of clean water, combined with intense heat, would lead to grasslands becoming deserts, wildfires spreading uncontrollably, and widespread global fatalities from dehydration and heat exhaustion.

> *And men were scorched with great heat, and they <u>blasphemed the name of God</u> who has power over these plagues; and they <u>did not repent</u> and give Him glory.*
>
> Revelation 16:9 (NKJV).

As suffering intensifies, the determination of the rebellion remaining on Earth strengthens and they curse God for such harsh plagues.

THE 5TH BOWL: DARKNESS & PAIN

> *Then the fifth angel poured out his bowl <u>on the throne of the beast</u>, and <u>his kingdom became full of darkness</u>; and they <u>gnawed their tongues</u> because of the pain.*
>
> Revelation 16:10 (NKJV).

While the 4th angel's bowl appears to have a global effect, the 5th angel's bowl specifically targets *"the throne of the beast,"* assaulting the heart of the Beast's kingdom and power. He and his followers are already *"full of darkness,"* both morally and spiritually, so this judgment must represent a more literal form of darkness. *"Gnawed their tongues in pain"* presents a particularly gruesome image that implies immense suffering and a type of madness, suggesting this experience transcends the mere loss of lighting and other electrical conveniences.

A collapse of their electrical grid could cripple the Beast's monetary system—likely a digital currency linked to a digital health ID. If the Beast's kingdom relied on AI and robotics, everything could go offline, possibly including the all-seeing image (idol) of the Beast erected in the **Temple.** With such dependence on technology, losing electrical power could create a metaphorical blindness, causing *"his kingdom to become full of darkness"* and the interruption would be felt worldwide.

Like the 4th angel's trumpet, this event parallels the 9th plague on Egypt, when God cast a *"darkness which may even be felt"* over the land for three days. This event seems to last much longer, as worshipers of the Beast are driven to a type of madness and continue to curse God in reaction to their afflictions.

THE 6TH BOWL: EUPHRATES DRIES UP

Then the sixth angel poured out his bowl <u>on the great river Euphrates</u>, and <u>its water was dried up</u>, so that the way of <u>the kings from the east</u> might be prepared.

Revelation 16:12 (NKJV).

The 6th angel's bowl judgment takes place at the Euphrates River, just as the 6th angel's trumpet did. When this verse was written in the first century, the

Euphrates divided East from West, marking the eastern boundary of Israel's inheritance. It served as a natural barrier against the kingdoms to the east, which today includes most of the Middle East, India, China, and Russia. Removing this barrier paves the way for an army invasion from *"the kings of the east."*

---

*And I saw <u>three unclean spirits like frogs</u> coming out of the mouth of the <u>dragon</u> [Satan], **out of the mouth of the <u>beast</u>, and out of the mouth of the <u>false prophet</u>**. For they are <u>spirits of demons, performing signs</u>, which go out to the <u>kings of the earth</u> and of the <u>whole world</u>, to <u>gather them to the battle</u> [of Armageddon] of <u>that great day of God</u> Almighty.*

Revelation 16:13–14 (NKJV).

"*Three unclean spirits*" emerge "*from the mouths*" of Satan, the Beast, and the False Prophet—a truly dark and unholy trinity. These spirits are "*like frogs,*" likely symbolizing their slimy nature, though we can easily imagine they resemble frogs (or alien grays?). They use their remarkable powers and influence to unite the world's armies and "*gather them*" for the **Battle of Armageddon...**

And they [the three spirits] <u>gathered them</u> [the world's armies] together to the place called in Hebrew, <u>Armageddon</u> [Megiddo].

Revelation 16:16 (NKJV).

THE BATTLE OF ARMAGEDDON

Great armies from the east and north, presumably Russia, China, and their Middle Eastern allies, join the armies of the 5th and 6th trumpets in the Valley of Megiddo, about 60 miles north of Jerusalem...

*Then you [Gog and Magog] **will come from your place out of the far north**, you and **many peoples** [nations] **with you, all of them riding on horses**, a great company and a **mighty army**.*

Ezekiel 38:15 (NKJV).

Russia and China boast significant horse populations, but it's unclear whether their armies are limited to *"riding on horses"* or if this is a primitive description due to its Old Testament origins. Modern warfare involves troop carriers that could be compared to equine as a mode of transportation. This *"mighty army"* is influenced by the Beast, though God assembles them near Jerusalem and permits them to execute a brutal attack on the city...

*For I [the Lord] **will gather all the nations to battle against Jerusalem**; The **city shall be taken**, The houses rifled, And the women ravished. **Half of the city shall go into captivity**, But the remnant of the people shall not be cut off from the city.*

Zechariah 14:2 (NKJV).

THE 7TH BOWL: THE FINAL JUDGMENT

Then the seventh angel poured out his bowl <u>into the air</u>, and a loud voice came out of the temple of heaven, <u>from the throne</u> [of God], saying, "<u>It is done!</u>"

Revelation 16:17 (NKJV).

The seventh angel's bowl compels God Himself to proclaim, *"It is done!"* These words resonate with Jesus' final words on the cross, *"It is finished!"* The last bowl of wrath has been poured out, and dire consequences await the Beast, the kings of the Earth, and their armies at the **Battle of Armageddon...**

And there were <u>noises and thunderings and lightnings</u>; and there was a <u>great earthquake</u>, such a mighty and great earthquake as had not occurred since men were on the earth. Now the <u>great city</u> [Jerusalem] was <u>divided into three parts</u>, and the <u>cities of the nations fell</u>. ...

Revelation 16:18–19 (NKJV).

Similar to the 7th seal and 7th trumpet, the 7th bowl unleashes *"noises and thunderings and lightnings."* It also causes an earthquake that shatters all previous records, and Jerusalem is *"divided into three parts."* The quake also devastates the cities of other nations, including Babylon...

5. God's Wrath

> *... And <u>great Babylon</u> was remembered before God, <u>to give her</u> the cup of the wine of <u>the fierceness of His wrath</u>. Then <u>every island fled away</u>, and the <u>mountains were not found</u>.*
>
> Revelation 16:19–20 (NKJV).

God turns His wrath towards *"great Babylon,"* and while specifics are lacking, the same earthquake seems to strike her capital, possibly Rome. The quake causes massive geological shifts, displacing islands and flattening mountains—perhaps hinting at colossal tsunamis. And just when it seems things couldn't worsen...

> *And <u>great hail</u> from heaven fell upon men, <u>each hailstone about the weight of a talent</u> [about 75 pounds]. <u>Men blasphemed God</u> because of the <u>plague of the hail</u>, since that plague was <u>exceedingly great</u>.*
>
> Revelation 16:21 (NKJV).

Like the 1st angel's trumpet, this event resembles the 7th plague on Egypt, when God caused *"great hail"* to fall over the battlefield. This time, however, the hail is significantly larger in size and destruction, with each hailstone weighing about 75 pounds—the unsaved curse God and His plagues for the last time. The armies gathered for the **Battle of Armageddon** are struck hard but not destroyed.

> "I will <u>shake heaven and earth</u>. I will <u>overthrow the throne of kingdoms</u>; I will destroy the strength of the <u>Gentile kingdoms</u>. I will <u>overthrow the chariots</u> and <u>those who ride in them</u>; The <u>horses and their riders shall come down</u>, Every one <u>by the sword of his brother</u> [attack one another]."
>
> Haggai 2:22 (NKJV).

God utterly devastates the armies of the kingdoms that have risen and allied against Him at the **Battle of Armageddon**. He instills a *"great panic"* that drives their soldiers mad, causing them to turn against one another. They *"overthrow the chariots"* and *"those who ride in them,"* alluding to the destruction of Pharaoh's army during the Exodus—possibly serving as another primitive description of modern warfare vehicles. Their armies are further diminished but still not annihilated.

THE FALL OF BABYLON

Babylon's rapid rise meets a swift decline. Her story is woven into the preceding pages, but we will summarize it here. The kings aligned with Babylon become drunk on power, and God *"puts it into their hearts"* to unite and *"make her desolate."* They further plunder their own economic systems to finance the Beast's military conquests...

5. God's Wrath

And the <u>ten horns</u> [kings] which you saw on the beast, these will hate the <u>harlot</u> [Babylon], <u>make her desolate and naked</u> [strip her riches], eat her flesh and burn her with fire [until nothing is left]. For <u>God has put it into their hearts to fulfill His purpose</u>, to be of <u>one mind</u> [united], and to <u>give their kingdom to the beast</u>, until the words of God are fulfilled.

Revelation 17:16–17 (NKJV).

Babylon is stripped of her wealth, resources, and influence. The Beast is given control of her kingdoms and armies. She loses her riches and social order, causing distress among those who profit from her affluence. The plight of trade merchants illustrates how the world was eager to support her as long as they were well compensated...

And the <u>merchants of the earth</u> will <u>weep and mourn over her</u> [Babylon], for <u>no one buys their merchandise</u> anymore: [...] For in one hour such great riches came to nothing.' Every shipmaster, all who travel by ship, sailors, and as many as trade on the sea, stood at a distance and cried out when they saw the smoke of her burning, saying, '<u>What is like this great city</u>?'

Revelation 18:11, 17–18 (NKJV).

The Beast gathers her armies to destroy Jerusalem and fight the Lord at the **Battle of Armageddon,** but God's judgments are decisive and swift....

> *Therefore her [Babylon's] <u>plagues will come in one day–death</u> and mourning and famine. And <u>she will be utterly burned with fire</u>, for <u>strong is the Lord God who judges her</u>.*
>
> Revelation 18:8 (NKJV).

Babylon's armies are significantly devastated in a remarkably short time, possibly *"in one day."* God's judgment of her is so strong that an angel of the Lord announces her defeat and calls out those who drank her wine and lusted for her riches...

> *And he [the angel] cried mightily with a loud voice, saying, <u>"Babylon the great is fallen, is fallen</u>, ... For <u>all the nations have drunk of the wine of the wrath of her fornication</u>, [temptations] the kings of the earth have committed fornication [lustful sin] with her, and the merchants of the earth <u>have become rich</u> through the <u>abundance of her luxury</u>."*
>
> Revelation 18:2–3 (NKJV).

God's judgments annihilate all but 1/6th of the Beast's armies, which could still amount to millions of troops assembled at the **Battle of Armageddon**. God directs their weary remnant south toward the mountains of Jerusalem, where they will soon confront Jesus and His army of angels and Saints. Get ready for the **Second Coming of Christ**—*the* **Apocalypse**.

THE SECOND COMING OF CHRIST (APOCALYPSE)

2300 days after the start of the **Great Tribulation** and 1040 days after the **Day of Christ** (Rapture), Jesus returns to Earth with His army of angels and Saints on white horses to fight at the **Battle of Armageddon.**

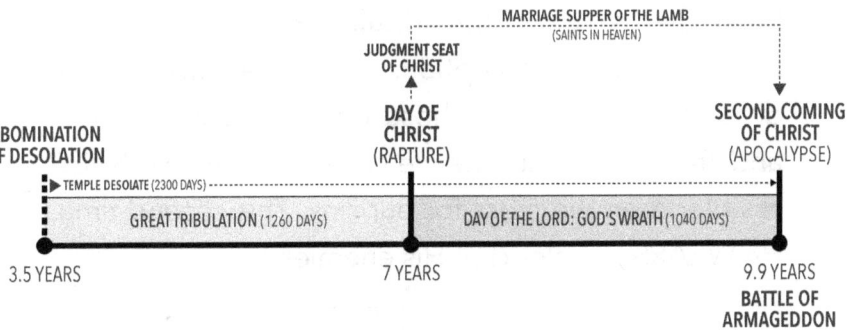

Also referred to as the Second Advent, the **Second Coming of Christ** (Apocalypse) is often confused with the **Day of Christ** (Rapture). The 2.9-year interval between these events is necessary for the fulfillment of the 7 trumpets and 7 bowls of **God's Wrath** (Judgment) on the world AFTER the Saints have been removed. On the **Day of Christ** (Rapture), Jesus came *"on the clouds"* to gather His Saints to Heaven—He did not descend to Earth. This time, during the **Second Coming of Christ** (Apocalypse), He returns to Earth WITH those Saints, riding *"on white horses"* to *"judge and make war"*...

> *Now I saw <u>heaven opened</u>, and behold, a <u>white horse</u>. And He who sat on him was called <u>Faithful and True</u> [Jesus], and in righteousness <u>He judges and makes war</u>.*
>
> Revelation 19:11 (NKJV).

We saw another white horse released when Jesus broke the 1st seal of the **Tribulation,** but its rider was given no such description. Here, we encounter a different white horse, whose rider is Jesus, *"Faithful and True."* The first time He came to Earth, He SHED His blood on the cross for our sins. This second time, He WEARS the blood of His enemies...

> **He was clothed with a <u>robe dipped in blood</u>, and His name is called <u>The Word of God</u>** [Jesus]. **And the <u>armies in heaven</u>,** [angels and Saints] **<u>clothed in fine linen</u>, white and clean, followed Him on <u>white horses</u>.**
>
> Revelation 19:13–14 (NKJV).

Since the **Day of Christ** (Rapture), a select number of Saints have been dining at the **Marriage Supper of the Lamb** in Heaven, *"clothed in fine linen."* Now, they join Jesus and His army of angels on white horses as they descend from Heaven to finish the **Battle of Armageddon.** Their numbers likely reach into the millions. One can imagine their lines extending out of sight and their rows stacked like sails on a ship. However arranged, they present a powerful and terrifying sight to their enemies, with Jesus leading their charge in His full glory and fury...

And I saw the <u>beast</u>, the <u>kings</u> of the earth, and <u>their armies</u>, gathered together <u>to make war against Him</u> [Jesus] who sat on the horse <u>and against His army</u> [of angels and Saints].

Revelation 19:19 (NKJV).

Jesus, along with His heavenly army of angels and Saints, is about to descend from Heaven to deliver the final blow to the Beast's rebellion. The stage is set for the return of the King...

And in that day His [Jesus'] <u>feet will stand on the Mount of Olives</u>, Which faces Jerusalem on the east. And the Mount of Olives <u>shall be split in two</u> [by a great earthquake], **From east to west, <u>Making a very large valley</u>; Half of the mountain shall move toward the north And half of it toward the south. Then you shall <u>flee through My mountain valley</u>,** ...

Zechariah 14:4–5 (NKJV).

When Jesus lands on the Mount of Olives, a powerful earthquake divides the mountain, forming a wide valley. This new valley offers an escape route for the captives of Jerusalem. A lot is happening in both the heavens and the Earth at this moment, and this is where we continue with the same "great earthquake" that occurs after the 7th bowl is poured out.

---

and I will <u>turn you around</u> and lead you on, bringing you up from the <u>far north</u>, [from Megiddo] and <u>bring you against the mountains of Israel</u>. [...] You shall fall upon the mountains of Israel, you and <u>all your troops</u> and the peoples who are with you [will be slain]

Ezekiel 39:2, 4 (NKJV).

God turns the remnants of the Beast's worn armies south toward the mountains of Israel, directly into the path of Jesus and His armies...

Now <u>out of His mouth</u> goes a <u>sharp sword</u> [His word], that with it He [Jesus] should <u>strike the nations</u>. And He Himself will rule them with a rod of iron. He Himself <u>treads the winepress</u> [smashes the grapes] of the fierceness and wrath of Almighty God.

Revelation 19:15 (NKJV).

Jesus's spoken word is like a "sharp sword." His pronouncement strikes the kingdoms of the nations allied against Him, destroying the remnants of their armies. His army of angels and Saints on horseback trample the battlefield like grapes in a winepress until it flows with blood. John's vision from an earlier chapter sums up everything...

5. God's Wrath

So He who sat on the cloud [Jesus] thrust in His sickle on the earth, and <u>the earth was reaped</u>. [...] and [the second angel] <u>gathered the vine of the earth</u> [the wicked], <u>and threw it into the great winepress of the wrath of God</u>. And the winepress was <u>trampled outside the city</u> [Jerusalem], and <u>blood came out of the winepress, up to the horses' bridles</u>, for one thousand six hundred furlongs [about 184 miles].

Revelation 14:16–20 (NKJV).

The prophet Zechariah includes unsettling details that appear to link the power of Christ's word to that of a nuclear weapon…

And this shall be the plague with which <u>the Lord will strike</u> all the people <u>who fought against Jerusalem</u>: Their <u>flesh shall dissolve</u> while they stand on their feet, Their <u>eyes shall dissolve</u> in their sockets, And their <u>tongues shall dissolve</u> in their mouths.

Zechariah 14:12 (NKJV).

After the annihilation of their armies, the Beast and the False Prophet are captured and *"cast alive into the lake of fire"*…

Then the <u>beast was captured</u>, and <u>with him the false prophet</u> who worked signs in his presence, by which he deceived those who <u>received the mark of the beast</u> and those who <u>worshiped</u>

his image. These two were <u>cast alive into the lake of fire</u> [hell] burning with brimstone.

Revelation 19:20 (NKJV).

This is the ultimate destination for all who reject Christ—and thus God. The *"lake of fire"* is *Gehenna*, commonly translated as *hell*. To this point, *Hades* remains the temporary destination for the unsaved dead. The Beast and the False Prophet are the FIRST cast into the *lake of fire*, with many more to follow.

The **Battle of Armageddon** has concluded. The Apocalypse is over, and the Lord has triumphed. Humanity's kingdoms have fallen, and evil has been defeated (for now).

SATAN SEALED IN THE BOTTOMLESS PIT

Then I saw <u>an angel</u> coming down from heaven, having <u>the key to the bottomless pit</u> and a <u>great chain</u> in his hand. He laid hold of the dragon, that serpent of old, who is the Devil and <u>Satan</u>, and <u>bound him for a thousand years</u>; [in the pit of the abyss]

Revelation 20:1–2 (NKJV).

Satan is subdued and locked in the bottomless pit by a mighty angel of God. It's unclear if this is the same angel who released the locust beasts at the 5th trumpet, but it's undoubtedly the same key and bottomless pit. This is the place that demons fear most; it is the *Abyss of Hades*—a dungeon prison where many fallen angels await the **Great White Throne Judgment**...

---

and **he** *[the angel] cast* **him** *[Satan]* **into the bottomless pit**, *and shut him up, and* **set a seal on him**, *so that he should deceive the nations* **no more till the thousand years were finished**. *But after these things [the 1000-year Millennium]* **he must be released for a little while**.

Revelation 20:3 (NKJV).

Surprisingly, Satan receives a 1000-year prison sentence instead of immediately joining the Beast and False Prophet in the *lake of fire (hell)*. It seems that God grants Satan one final opportunity to repent —or at least 1000 years to think about it.

CHRIST'S JUDGMENT OF THE NATIONS

The armies that marched with the Beast have been destroyed. Nevertheless, the nations of those armies and their surviving populations remain accountable for their transgressions against God and Jerusalem...

I will also **gather all nations**, *and bring them down to the* **Valley of Jehoshaphat**; *and I will enter into* **judgment with them there**

Joel 3:2 (NKJV).

Jehoshaphat means "Yahweh (God) judges." Geographically, the *"Valley of Jehoshaphat"* is likely the Kidron Valley, located on the east side of Jerusalem. Here, the surviving populations of *"all the nations"* are gathered for judgment...

---

*"**All the nations** [all people] **will be <u>gathered before Him</u>** [Jesus], and He will <u>separate them</u> one from another, as a shepherd divides his <u>sheep from the goats</u>. And He will set the <u>sheep on His right hand</u>, but the <u>goats on the left</u>. Then the King will say to those on His right hand, 'Come, you blessed of My Father, <u>inherit the kingdom</u> prepared for you from the foundation of the world:"* [–Jesus]

Matthew 25:32–34 (NKJV).

The *"sheep on His right hand"* repented AFTER the **Rapture** and likely BEFORE the **Second Coming of Christ** (Apocalypse). They *"inherit the kingdom"* of God for eternity, but continue to live out extended mortal lives during the **Millennium.**

"Then He [Jesus] will also say to those <u>on the left hand</u> ["goats"], 'Depart from Me, you <u>cursed, into the everlasting fire</u> prepared for the devil and his angels: [...] And these ["goats"] will go away into <u>everlasting punishment</u>, but the righteous ["sheep"] into <u>eternal life</u>." [–Jesus]

Matthew 25:41, 46 (NKJV).

The *"goats on the left hand"* likely refers to the unsaved survivors who FAILED to repent before the **Second Coming of Christ** (Apocalypse). They likely worshiped the Beast, took his mark, and cursed God for their afflictions. The time for their mortal judgment is at hand, and they are *"cursed into the everlasting fire."* Previously, the Beast and False Prophet were the first to be *"cast alive into the lake of fire."* The distinction between *"cursed into..."* and *"cast alive into..."* may indicate that these unsaved survivors experience a mortal death (now or in the near future) and their souls are temporarily sent to *Hades* —along with the unsaved dead throughout history— to await the Second Resurrection to physically stand before the Lord for the **Great White Throne Judgment** at the end of the **Millennium.**

CHAPTER 6
THE DAY OF THE LORD: THE MILLENNIUM

The first part of the **Day of the Lord: God's Wrath** (Judgment), lasted 1040 days (2.9 years). The second part, the **Millennium,** continues for the next 997.1 years. **God's Millennial Kingdom** has completely replaced man's earthly kingdoms, and the Lord now dwells with humanity as initially intended. The **Millennium** is a time of restoration, peace, and blessing on Earth.

THE EARTH & JERUSALEM RESTORED

By the start of the **Millennium,** the Earth is in rough shape. It has recently been devastated by warfare, earthquakes, tsunamis, tectonic shifts, volcanoes, lightning storms, scorching heat, fires, droughts, giant hail, and meteor impacts—all on a global scale. Cities fell, countrysides burned, seaports and islands disappeared, and mountains flattened. Oceans, seas, lakes, rivers, and springs were poisoned. The stars, sun, and moon were repeatedly cloaked in darkness. Agriculture has been effectively paralyzed, and the loss of life from numerous wars is colossal. The population of Earth may have been reduced by over 90%. Now is the time for restoration, starting with Israel. It's time to cleanse the **Temple** and rebuild Jerusalem.

When Jesus returned to Earth, He touched down on the Mount of Olives, splitting the mountain from east to west. The two halves moved north and south, opening up a large valley. A great spring of *"living waters"* opened beneath Jerusalem, creating crystal-clear rivers that restore the region's seas…

And in that day it shall be that <u>living waters</u> [springs] shall <u>flow from Jerusalem</u>, half of them <u>toward the eastern sea</u> [Dead Sea] and half of them <u>toward the western sea</u> [Mediterranean Sea]; in both summer and winter it shall occur.

Zechariah 14:8 (NKJV).

The Jordan Valley fills to form an enormous lake and a grand canal connects the Dead Sea to the Red Sea, transforming Jerusalem into a seaport. The barren desert becomes a fertile landscape…

… For waters [springs] **shall <u>burst forth in the wilderness</u>, and <u>streams in the desert</u>. The parched ground** [barren desert] **shall**

6. The Millennium

become a pool [lake]*, and the thirsty land springs of water; in the habitation of jackals, where each lay, there shall be grass with reeds and rushes* [marshes]*.*

Isaiah 35:6–7 (NKJV).

Most books of the Bible refer to the eastern Mediterranean region, but we can safely assume that the geological healing is felt globally. Storms are calmed, and a mild, temperate climate rests over the Earth. There is neither summer nor winter, nor day nor night.

It shall come to pass in that day *[Day of the Lord] that there will be no [sun]* light; The lights *[sunlight and moonlight]* will diminish. It shall be* one day *which is known to the Lord–neither day nor night. But* at evening time *it shall happen That* it will be light.

Zechariah 14:6–7 (NKJV).

The environment is perfect, both physically and spiritually. There is no famine, illness, or disease, and those with ailments are healed…

Then the eyes of the blind shall be opened**, and the ears of the deaf** shall be unstopped **[opened]. Then the lame [disabled]** shall leap like a deer**, And the tongue of the dumb [challenged]** sing**. …**

Isaiah 35:5–6 (NKJV).

During the **Millennium,** the faithful Saints lead simpler, more sustainable lives. They construct their own houses and cultivate their own food. Their gardens flourish abundantly, and *"the work of their hands"* is enjoyable and rewarding...

They shall <u>build houses</u> and <u>inhabit them</u>; They shall <u>plant vineyards</u> and <u>eat their fruit</u>. They shall not build and another inhabit; They shall not plant and another eat; For as <u>the days of a tree</u> [hundreds of years], so shall be <u>the days of My people</u>, And My elect [Saints] shall long <u>enjoy the work of their hands</u>. They shall <u>not labor in vain</u>, [without result]...

Isaiah 65:21–23 (NKJV).

The mortal Saints live greatly extended lives, likened to *"the days of a tree."* This time of peace and blessings also extends to the animals. Carnivores turn into vegetarians, predators cease hunting, and their former prey shares their land and dens...

<u>The wolf</u> also shall dwell [in peace] with the lamb, <u>The leopard</u> shall lie down [rest] with the <u>young goat</u>, The <u>calf and the young lion and the fatling</u> [gather] <u>together</u> [without issue]; And a little child shall lead [drive/herd] them. The <u>cow and the bear shall graze</u> [together in the pasture]; Their young ones shall lie down together; And the <u>lion shall eat straw like the ox</u>.

Isaiah 11:6–7 (NKJV).

6. The Millennium

Humans no longer need to fear ferocious animals, nor do animals need to fear humans, as we also return to vegetarian (or perhaps pescatarian) diets. Domestic animals and more exotic creatures are kept for mutual enjoyment. Livestock is still raised and herded for various agricultural purposes, like wool and dairy, and unlikely species cohabitation is no longer a safety concern. The Earth is so safe that there is no worry about biting, stinging, or poisonous creatures like snakes, spiders, and insects…

The nursing <u>child shall play by the cobra's hole</u> [without danger], And the weaned <u>child shall put his hand in the viper's den</u> [without getting bit].

Isaiah 11:8 (NKJV).

This restored land, with its temperate climate, fresh waters, lush vegetation, and the peaceful coexistence of humans and animals, resembles the *Garden of Eden* that God initially designed before sin entered the Earth. However, life in the **Millennium** is not without sin. Free will persists as new generations choose their own paths, yet the highest authority, Jesus, reigns over this new world along with His appointed elect of elder and martyred Saints from the **Church Age.**

THE MARTYRS REIGN

And I saw <u>thrones</u> [on Earth], and they [Church elders] <u>sat on them, and <u>judgment</u> [authority] <u>was committed to them</u>. Then I saw the souls of those [martyred Saints] who had been <u>beheaded for their witness to Jesus</u> and for the word of God, who had <u>not worshiped the beast or his image</u>, and had <u>not received his mark</u> on their foreheads or on their hands [during the Tribulation]. And they <u>lived and reigned with Christ for a thousand years</u> [in God's Millennial Kingdom].

Revelation 20:4 (NKJV).

In this vision, we again see the martyred Saints of the **Tribulation** singled out. They were awarded authority (at the **Judgment Seat of Christ**) to *"live and reign with Christ for a thousand years"* on Earth until the end of the **Millennium.** They were resurrected at the end of the **Great Tribulation** on the **Day of Christ** (Rapture), in the SECOND STAGE of the FIRST RESURRECTION.

But <u>the rest of the dead did not live again</u> [resurrect] <u>until the thousand years</u> [of the Millennium] <u>were finished</u>. This is the [third stage of the] <u>first resurrection</u>. Blessed and holy is he who has part in the <u>first resurrection</u>. Over such the <u>second death</u> [hell] <u>has no power</u>, ...

Revelation 20:5–6 (NKJV).

6. The Millennium

It appears that many souls are waiting in Heaven and *Hades* at this time, but they do not *"live again"* (resurrect) until the end of the **Millennium** to physically stand before the Lord at the **Great White Throne Judgment**. The resurrection terminology in this section is a bit tricky, so we'll clarify it here.

THE FIRST & SECOND RESURRECTIONS

Everyone who has ever lived on Earth is appointed to *"die once"* (a mortal death) and later receive their eternal judgment from God.

And as it is appointed for <u>men to die once</u>, but after this the [Great White Throne] <u>judgment</u>, ...

Hebrews 9:27 (NKJV).

Everyone is part of either the FIRST or SECOND RESURRECTION to receive their glorified spiritual bodies, enabling them to physically stand before God at the **Great White Throne Judgment**. The First Resurrection is for all SAVED believers (Saints) and occurs in THREE STAGES over thousands of years.

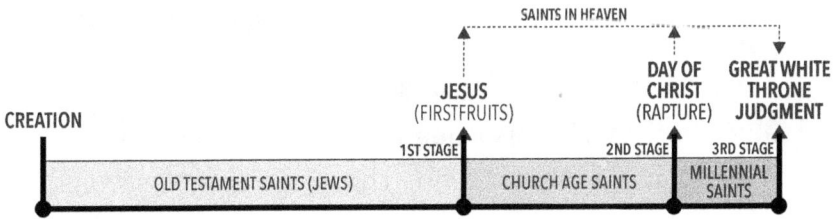

> *But now **Christ is risen from the dead** [resurrected], and has become the **firstfruits** of those [Old Testament Saints (Jews)] who have **fallen asleep** [died]. For since by man [sin] **came death**, by Man also came the **resurrection of the dead**. For as **in Adam all die**, even so **in Christ all shall be made alive**.*
>
> 1 Corinthians 15:20-22 (NKJV).

The FIRST STAGE of the First Resurrection, also known as the *Resurrection of Life*, began when Jesus was resurrected into His glorified spiritual body 3 days after His crucifixion. He was immediately followed by the resurrection of the Old Testament Saints (Jews), who secured their salvation by obeying God's laws. They ascended to Heaven in their glorified spiritual bodies, but many of them took a stroll through Jerusalem first...

> *... and **the graves were opened**; and **many bodies of the saints** [Old Testament Jews] who had **fallen asleep** [died] were **raised** [resurrected]; and **coming out of the graves** after His [Jesus'] **resurrection**, they went **into the holy city** [Jerusalem] and appeared to many.*
>
> Matthew 27:52-53 (NKJV).

Their appearance is similar to how Jesus physically appeared to His Apostles and others during the 40 days after His resurrection. These are the *"firstfruits"*

6. The Millennium

of the First Resurrection, and they physically reside in Heaven today. The SECOND STAGE of the First Resurrection occurs at the end of the **Great Tribulation** on the **Day of Christ** (Rapture) and encompasses all the Saints of the **Church Age**...

But each one <u>in his own order</u>: Christ the <u>firstfruits</u> [First Stage], afterward those who are Christ's <u>at His coming</u> [Second Stage].

1 Corinthians 15:23 (NKJV).

Some Saints of the **Church Age** are rewarded with authority to reign with Christ in **God's Millennial Kingdom** on Earth for almost 1000 years. The rest of them will physically reside in Heaven during the **Millennium**. The THIRD STAGE of the First Resurrection occurs at the end of the **Millennium** and encompasses all the Saints who were saved AFTER the **Day of Christ** (Rapture)...

---

*Then comes <u>the end</u> [Third Stage], when He [Jesus] **delivers the** [Millennial] **kingdom** [on Earth] **to God the Father, when He puts an end to all** [of man's] **rule and all authority and power. For He** [Jesus] **must reign till He has put all enemies under His feet.***

1 Corinthians 15:24–25 (NKJV).

Many of these Saints were likely killed during the 2.9 years of **God's Wrath.** Those who survived and passed **Christ's Judgment of the Nations** live well into the **Millennium**. Upon their death, their souls will wait in Heaven until the end of the **Millennium** for their physical resurrection into their glorified spiritual bodies (the THIRD STAGE). The Saints that live to the end of the **Millennium** are presumably raptured (and resurrected) as part of the THIRD STAGE as well. All the SAVED believers (Saints of the Old Testament, the **Church Age**, and the **Millennium**) are included in one of the THREE STAGES of the FIRST RESURRECTION, and all are guaranteed salvation to eternal life with God.

The SECOND RESURRECTION, also called the *Resurrection of the Damned*, is specifically for the UNSAVED and occurs ONCE at the end of the **Millennium**. It includes all of the unsaved who died throughout history and through the end of the **Millennium**, and their souls wait in *Hades* until they are resurrected to physically stand before the Lord at the **Great White Throne Judgment**. The UNSAVED living at the end of the **Millennium** are presumably raptured (and resurrected) for the same purpose. All the UNSAVED of the SECOND RESURRECTION will ultimately experience the *"second death"*—a spiritual death for those condemned to the *lake of fire* at the **Great White Throne Judgment**.

GOD'S MILLENNIAL KINGDOM

It seems there are two distinct types, or classes, living on Earth during the **Millennium:**

1. Immortal Saints (who reign with Christ)
2. Mortal survivors (and their generations)

The mortal survivors repented and passed **Christ's Judgment of the Nations.** Though they have secured their eternal salvation, they may ultimately experience mortal deaths during the **Millennium.** However, God significantly extends their lifespans to hundreds of years, similar to that of the early biblical patriarchs…

No more shall an infant from there live but a few days [due to sickness], *Nor an old man who has not fulfilled his days* [due to a premature death]; **For <u>the child shall die one hundred years old</u>,** [an untimely death] **But the sinner being one hundred years old shall be accursed** [to die of old age].

Isaiah 65:20 (NKJV).

An untimely (tragic) death at 100 years is regarded as a young death comparable to that of a child. However, the unsaved (from successive generations) are cursed to die before reaching the age of 100, much like today.

All of Earth's inhabitants live under the authority of Christ as their King, but the immortal Saints are given regional jurisdiction to rule over the mortal survivors and their descendants. Mortal children, born throughout the **Millennium,** have the personal responsibility to exercise their faith in the Lord—just like all people from past ages—and many choose to reject Christ as their savior.

Since the immortal Saints *"shall be priests of God and of Christ,"* we can assume they do not marry or reproduce. They were wed to Christ at the **Marriage Supper of the Lamb** and given glorified spiritual bodies like the angels. Mixing their seed with mortals is strictly prohibited by God, as noted in Genesis 6.

Among the mortal survivors are the 144,000 Jews —likely a much greater number representing all Jews at this point—who were sealed from harm during **God's Wrath** (Judgment). They live to see the restoration of their nation of Israel, exalted to its fullest glory with Christ as their King, reigning from the *Throne of David* in Jerusalem as prophesied. They, too, experience considerably extended lifespans in the **Millennium** and produce multiple generations of children. Most Jews reside in Jerusalem and enjoy preferred status, but they likely do not reign with Christ, as do the immortal Saints.

NATIONS WORSHIP THE KING

Just as Christians today, many Millennial Saints view a trip to Israel as both a celebration and an essential expression of their faith, and they make regular pilgrimages to Jerusalem to honor their Lord…

> **Many people** shall come and say, "Come, and <u>let us go up to the mountain of the Lord</u>, To the <u>house of the God of Jacob</u> [Jerusalem]; **He** [Jesus] <u>will teach us His ways</u>, And we shall <u>walk in His paths</u>." For out of <u>Zion shall go forth the law</u>, And the <u>word of the Lord from Jerusalem</u>.
>
> Isaiah 2:3 (NKJV).

Those who belonged to the nations that fought against Israel are specifically obligated to make an annual pilgrimage to Jerusalem to present their tithes and offerings at the Temple, honor the Lord, and express gratitude for His ongoing blessings and provisions. This is likely a generational obligation…

> And it shall come to pass that <u>everyone who is left</u> [after the judgment] <u>of all the nations which came against Jerusalem</u> shall go up [to Jerusalem] from <u>year to year to worship the King</u>, the Lord of hosts, and to <u>keep the Feast of Tabernacles</u>.
>
> Zechariah 14:16 (NKJV).

Those who do not make their required pilgrimage to Jerusalem to honor the Lord bring a curse of drought upon their communities...

*And it shall be that **whichever of the families** [peoples/tribes/nations] of the earth **do not come up to Jerusalem** to **worship the King** [Jesus], the Lord of hosts, **on them there will be no rain** [drought].*

Zechariah 14:17 (NKJV).

While this "plague" may appear mild compared to the plagues of **God's Wrath** (Judgment), agriculture remains a vital component of every community in the **Millennium,** and any lack of harvest serves as a strong incentive to rectify their transgression.

CHRIST'S REIGN ON EARTH

After 6000 years, man's appointed reign ends and is replaced by **God's Millennial Kingdom** on Earth. Jesus reigns from the *Throne of David* in Jerusalem for the next 997.1 years. All false religions and pagan spiritualism are eliminated, and Satan is locked in the bottomless pit. The name of Jesus is the one truth that unites the entire world. In Christ, all distinctions between Jew and Gentile vanish, as do those between race, creed, and nationality...

6. The Millennium

And the Lord will be <u>king over the whole earth</u>. In that day [Day of the Lord] *it shall be–"<u>The Lord is one</u>," And <u>His name one</u>.*

Zechariah 14:9 (NKJV).

Although His holy righteousness prevails, free will persists, and sin occasionally erupts. Crimes like theft and violence are swiftly suppressed by the Lord's regional magistrates, the immortal Saints...

Behold, a king [Jesus] *will <u>reign in righteousness</u>* [over the Earth], *and* [His] *<u>princes</u>* [the Saints] *<u>will rule with justice</u>.*

Isaiah 32:1 (NKJV).

Jesus Himself directly addresses global issues. His rule is divine, and His justice remains unwavering. However, He is not one to be tested, and He governs the nations *"with a rod of iron"*...

... And <u>He Himself</u> [Jesus] *<u>will rule them</u>* [the nations] *with a <u>rod of iron</u>. ...*

Revelation 19:15 (NKJV).

Jesus alone is worthy of this responsibility. He alone cannot be corrupted by such power—an impossible role for any man or "Beast." As ruler and judge of all nations, His justice is decisive and fair, and His authority is unquestionable...

> *He [Jesus] shall <u>judge between the nations</u>, And <u>rebuke many people</u>; They shall beat [forge] their <u>swords into plowshares</u>, And their <u>spears into pruning hooks</u>; Nation shall not lift up sword against nation, <u>Neither shall they learn war anymore</u>.*
>
> Isaiah 2:4 (NKJV).

There is such peace between the nations that people recycle their weapons of war and self-defense into more practical items, such as farming tools—or, metaphorically speaking, into decisive instruments that cut the roots and offshoots of problems before they grow out of control.

SATAN RELEASED FROM THE BOTTOMLESS PIT

By the end of the 1000-year **Millennium,** the Earth is fully repopulated. Given the absence of war, violent crime, famine, disease, natural disasters, and significantly extended lifespans, this repopulation is not difficult to envision. In 1000 years, over 40 generations could emerge—each with their own unique perspectives on society, culture, and religion. Simply stating that these generational aspects have changed for us in the past 100 years is a gross understatement, not to mention the changes over the past 1000 years when the Roman Byzantine Empire thrived.

6. The Millennium

During this time, Satan is sealed in the bottomless pit, unable to spread his influence and deceit. While the immortal and Millennial Saints undoubtedly understand the chaos he caused and the threat he poses if released, it requires no stretch of imagination to consider generations upon generations that scoff at such arcane beliefs. By the time Satan is *"released from his prison,"* there could be potentially hundreds of millions of people who marvel at his appearance, readily absorb his lies, and are deceived into following his leadership as many did during the 7-year **Tribulation...**

Now when the <u>thousand years have expired</u>, Satan will be <u>released from his prison</u> and will go out to <u>deceive the nations</u> which are in the four corners of the earth [all the nations], <u>Gog and Magog</u>, to <u>gather them together to battle</u>, whose number is as <u>the sand of the sea</u>.

Revelation 20:7–8 (NKJV).

This is not the same *"Gog and Magog"* armies that fought at the **Battle of Armageddon**—they were annihilated by Christ almost 1000 years ago. In this context, *"Gog and Magog"* represent an equally vicious rebellion under the influence of Satan, comprised of armies from all nations and likely in greater numbers.

SATAN'S FINAL REBELLION

> ***They** [Satan's armies] **went up on the breadth** [both sides] **of the earth** [broad plain] **and <u>surrounded the camp</u> of the saints and the <u>beloved city</u>** [Jerusalem]. **And <u>fire came down from God</u> out of heaven and <u>devoured them</u>.***
>
> Revelation 20:9 (NKJV).

Not much has been written about this final rebellion. Satan's armies surround Jerusalem, and they are swiftly devoured by fire from God. While their demise is abrupt, Satan's buildup likely takes a few years. Deceiving nations, creating allies, making battle plans, and deploying armies require time, suggesting that Satan may use his playbook from the 7-year **Tribulation**. Predictably, the result remains the same; and perhaps this is the point. It seems that no matter the evidence—even after ten centuries of peace and righteousness—people still choose to rebel against the Lord and reject the salvation of Christ out of pride and love for themselves. These rebels will soon face eternal judgment, but for Satan, that time is now…

> ***The devil, who deceived them, was <u>cast into the lake of fire</u> and brimstone** [hell] **where the <u>beast and the false prophet are</u>. And they will be <u>tormented day and night</u> forever and ever.***
>
> Revelation 20:10 (NKJV).

Satan becomes the third member *"cast into the lake of fire."* He does not rule in hell, as portrayed in lore and movies. Instead, he is subject to the same fate as the Beast, the False Prophet, and every condemned inhabitant for eternity, although varying levels of severity appear to exist.

CHAPTER 7
THE NEW HEAVEN & EARTH

THE GREAT WHITE THRONE JUDGMENT

Commonly referred to as "Judgment Day," the **Great White Throne Judgment** signifies the end of the **Day of the Lord,** the end of our prophetic timeline, and the end of time as we know it. From this point on, there is only eternity...

Then I saw a <u>great white throne</u> and <u>Him who sat on it</u> *[Jesus],* from whose face *[presence]* <u>the earth and the heaven fled away</u>. And there was found <u>no place</u> *[location]* for them.

Revelation 20:11 (NKJV).

Jesus sits on a white throne to deliver the final judgment to everyone who lived on Earth and all who rebelled against God in Heaven. Only the loyal and steadfast angels are exempt from this judgment, though they are present as witnesses. The throne that John sees in his vision is neither in Heaven nor on Earth, as both realms have been defiled and must be cleansed and renewed. Their inhabitants are removed to prepare the **New Heaven and Earth** (the next chapter). Considering how long it might take to judge billions of people, it's certain that this event occurs in eternity (outside of time as we know it). We'll all be there, but we won't have to wait long for our turn—since there is *no time to wait in!*

And I saw <u>the dead, small and great</u>, [of the First Resurrection] <u>standing before God</u> [Jesus], and <u>books</u> [of deeds] <u>were opened</u>. And another book was opened, which is the <u>Book of Life</u> [eternal salvation]. And the dead were <u>judged according to their works</u>, by the things which were <u>written in the books</u>.

Revelation 20:12 (NKJV).

"The dead, small and great," likely refers to all the Saints from the FIRST RESURRECTION (see Chapter 6: The First & Second Resurrections). They have been resurrected in THREE STAGES and transformed into their glorified spiritual bodies to physically *"stand before God"* at the **Great White Throne Judgment.** They are *"judged according to their works"* by the accounts *"written in the books."* Every word, deed, and thought of their lives has been accurately recorded. The Lord's justice is beyond reproach in His holy courtroom, and the recorded evidence is read from the books for all to hear.

7. The New Heaven & Earth

Because all have sinned and no one can earn their way into Heaven, only the faithful Saints listed in the Book of Life are spared from the *lake of fire*. Their eternal salvation is secure, but their recorded actions (and inactions) will influence their roles in the **New Heaven and Earth**.

> *The sea gave up the dead who were in it, and Death and Hades delivered up the dead who were in them [the Second Resurrection]. And they were judged, each one according to his works.*
>
> Revelation 20:13 (NKJV).

"The sea" signifies the source of earthly rebellion, yet one cannot help but associate the fabled *Davey Jones's Locker* with *Hades*—the realm of the dead. The imprisoned captives of *"Death and Hades"* are *"delivered up"* in the SECOND RESURRECTION for their time of judgment. This exhumation includes the fallen angels and demons sealed in the bottomless pit—the *Abyss of Hades*—and all are *"cast into the lake of fire"* (hell)...

> *Then [those from] Death and Hades were cast into the lake of fire. This is the second death. And anyone not found written in the Book of Life was cast into the lake of fire [hell].*
>
> Revelation 20:14 (NKJV).

The *"second death"* is an eternal death for those *"not found written in the Book of Life."* While the *lake of fire* is aptly named and biblically described as a *"blazing furnace; burning brimstone; and sulfur,"* the implied fire likely serves as a metaphor for God's judgment and punishment, although unrelenting heat and thirst appear to play a role.

Hell is a place of *torment*—not torture. Those exiled there endure an eternity of consciousness to reflect on their guilt and shame for rejecting God. They suffer forever from the emptiness of their complete separation from Him and any form of goodness. If tossed into a fiery furnace, there would be no thoughts of reflection or feelings of emptiness—only pain and panic from torture.

The Bible does not offer many details about the *lake of fire (hell)* or its location. Many believe it is situated deep within the Earth, where magma flows under intense pressure and heat. However, this theory seems implausible if its inhabitants retain physical bodies in any form from the Second Resurrection. In the book of Matthew, Jesus refers to *hell* as the *"outer darkness"* three different times. In Greek, this can be translated as "the utmost farthest place," possibly beyond our universe, such as a black hole or another dimension. Wherever *hell* is located, we are told it is a physical place—not a self-imposed

7. The New Heaven & Earth

prison of the mind or spirit. After all of the individual judgments are completed...

The <u>last enemy</u> that will be destroyed is <u>death</u>.

---

1 Corinthians 15:26 (NKJV).

As we discussed earlier, *"death"* referred to the rider of the pale horse, released when Jesus broke the seal of the 4th Holy Scroll during the **Tribulation.** While this imagery conveys a significant story and seems to align with various mythologies and figures in popular fiction, such as the "Grim Reaper" or "Angel of Death," there is no Scripture that directly supports the idea of *Death* being an angel, demon, spirit, or entity. Similar to the riders of the red and black horses, they are more likely to be God's angels (messengers) delivering the opened scrolls to Earth, each one removing another level of protection. *Death* was introduced to the Earth when humanity first sinned, becoming both a condition in life and a curse in eternity. When Jesus removes *Death*, He abolishes the final penalty of sin, which, in turn, removes sin itself. *Death* is *"destroyed"* before the establishment of the **New Heaven and Earth,** ensuring the eternal Kingdom of God is free from sin, death, descent, and rebellion.

THE NEW HEAVEN & EARTH

"For behold, I create <u>new heavens</u> and a <u>new earth</u>; And the former shall <u>not be remembered</u> or come to mind."

Isaiah 65:17 (NKJV).

If one is counting, this is the third major construction (or reconstruction) of the Earth: 1) at **Creation,** 2) after the flood, and 3) as we enter the eternal state. John views God's completed works as his vision continues in Revelation...

Now I saw a <u>new heaven</u> and a <u>new earth</u>, for the <u>first heaven and the first earth had passed</u> [gone] away. Also there was <u>no more sea</u>.

Revelation 21:1 (NKJV).

The **New Heaven and Earth** replace the first in a material sense. *"The sea"* once more signifies the source of worldly rebellion and chaos. These behaviors and sins are eliminated, though the literal seas likely remain in some form. The **New Earth** arises as God initially intended...

And I heard a loud voice from heaven saying, "Behold, the tabernacle [dwelling place] **of <u>God is with men</u>, and <u>He will dwell</u>**

7. The New Heaven & Earth

with them, and they shall be His people. <u>God Himself will be with them</u> and be their God."

Revelation 21:3 (NKJV).

New Heaven and Earth are now one and the same. The *Garden of Eden* and humanity's communion with God have been restored. This is the ultimate promise of His covenant. He is *"Immanuel, God with us"* for all eternity...

"And <u>God will wipe away every tear</u> from their eyes; there shall be <u>no more death</u>, <u>nor sorrow</u>, <u>nor crying</u>. There shall be <u>no more pain</u>, for <u>the former things have passed</u> [gone] away."

Revelation 21:4 (NKJV).

The **New Earth** is free from sorrow, suffering, pain, and death, because all of creation is liberated from the consequences of man's sin for eternity. Even nature is released from the curse of sin. All things in Heaven and Earth are renewed...

Then He who <u>sat on the throne</u> [Jesus] said, "Behold, <u>I make all things new</u>. [...] <u>It is done!</u> I am the Alpha and the Omega, the Beginning and the End." [–Jesus]

Revelation 21:5–6 (NKJV).

Jesus's words echo the pronouncements from Heaven's throne at the final release of God's judgments, stating, *"It is done!"* Those who chose mortal sin over eternal life have been cast into the *lake of fire* (the Second Death), and the salvation of His Saints is secured. The angels and Saints leave the **Great White Throne Judgment** and enter their new home for eternity.

NEW JERUSALEM

The entire Earth is now God's garden paradise—*Eden restored.* He places the crown jewel on His creation, crafted by His hands. A magnificent city for His people. A wedding gift for the Bride of the Lamb. John's vision continues…

And he [the angel] **carried me away <u>in the Spirit</u>** [vision] **to a <u>mountain great and high</u>, and showed me <u>the Holy City</u>,** [new] **Jerusalem, <u>coming down out of heaven from God</u>,**

Revelation 21:10 (NKJV).

From the mountaintop, John enjoys a breathtaking view of **New Jerusalem** descending from the heavens and establishing its permanent home on **New Earth.** He perceives remarkable details of its divine construction does his best to describe what he sees in terms we can comprehend…

7. The New Heaven & Earth

...having <u>the glory of God</u>. <u>Her light was like a most precious stone</u>, like a <u>jasper</u> stone [multiple colors], <u>clear as crystal</u>. Also she had a great and <u>high wall with twelve gates</u>, and <u>twelve angels at the gates</u>, and <u>names written on them</u>, which are the names of the <u>twelve tribes of the children of Israel</u>

Revelation 21:11–12 (NKJV).

John compares the city's walls and streets to precious stones and metals, all possessing the transparent quality of crystal. The single source of illumination in the city is *"the glory of God,"* which generates an iridescent display of refracting colors and light from every surface. The rebellion has been vanquished, and the 12 gates remain open; however, 12 angels guard them as symbols of security, strength, and remembrance. Each gate is inscribed with the names of the 12 tribes of Israel, presumably one name per gate.

Now the wall of the city had <u>twelve foundations</u>, and on them were <u>the names of the twelve apostles</u> of the Lamb [Jesus].

Revelation 21:14 (NKJV)

The wall's foundations bear the names of the 12 Apostles of Christ. This memorial declares that Old Testament Jews and New Testament Christians are sanctified and united for eternity under the Lord.

The twelve gates were twelve pearls: *each individual gate was [made]* ***of one pearl.*** *And **the street of the city was pure gold**, like **transparent glass**.*

Revelation 21:21 (NKJV).

Each gate is crafted from a single pearl, as best John can describe, again alluding to their beauty and iridescence. This description has given rise to the cliché of the "pearly gates" often used to depict Heaven's entrance. John compares the streets to *"pure gold,"* perhaps as a tribute to the righteous path of the city's inhabitants. Like the walls, the streets exhibit a transparent quality.

*The city is **laid out as a square**; its length is as great as its breadth. And he [the angel] **measured the city** with the reed: twelve thousand [12,000] furlongs [1380 miles]. Its **length, breadth, and height are equal**.*

Revelation 21:16 (NKJV).

The new city's base is *"laid out as a square,"* measuring *"12,000 furlongs."* If this is a literal measurement, it would equal 1,380 miles (2,220 kilometers), the distance from New York City to Dallas. An equal height would breach the exosphere well into the realm of satellites, creating an actual "stairway to heaven." Nothing is impossible for God, but this scale is beyond human comprehension. As we've observed in other scriptures, the number 12,000 can also represent completeness and perfection, which is certainly applicable here. The unit of measurement comes from the Greek word "stadion," which can also refer to a stadium or arena. When John writes this, the Romans have probably constructed over 100 magnificent stadiums and arenas in the Mediterranean region, making this a powerful analogy for the time. The measurement of 12,000 may indicate that it is, indeed, quite enormous. The question may simply be, *"How enormous?"*

John notes that *"its length, breadth, and height are equal,"* which would liken it to a cube in shape—the most popular interpretation. However, there is another basic shape with a square base and an equal height: a pyramid. So why didn't John say "pyramid" in his description? In fairness, he didn't say "cube" either. He provides basic proportions; the rest is open to interpretation, so let's explore these possibilities. A cubic shape would compare **New Jerusalem** to the Borg ship from the Star Trek: The Next Generation series or perhaps the Muslim Kaaba in Mecca—both interesting but completely uninspiring and devoid of God's divine creativity.

A pyramid shape makes more sense in both function and aesthetics. This theory is intriguing for several reasons: 1) ancient pyramids are found worldwide with no apparent connections, suggesting divine inspiration; 2) many ancient pyramids feature a flat top and include a large plateau, typically the site of a temple or shrine; 3) ancient pyramids were not the smooth representations we envision today—instead, their surface comprises graduated steps or levels. These are all characteristics of a "ziggurat," a step pyramid made up of concentric levels that ascend to a plateau, often featuring a primary staircase cut into the center of one or more sides.

King Nebuchadnezzar is credited with building the fabled "Hanging Gardens of Babylon"—one of the Seven Wonders of the World—around 600 BC. The gardens did not actually "hang" but were a series of terraces and roof gardens integrated into a ziggurat structure with a complex irrigation system flowing from its apex. Interestingly, every culture associates gardens and flowing waters with divinity, and mountains are seen as places to commune with the heavens. A mountain garden motif, replete with flowing waters, is a universal theme of divine inspiration, with many historical examples, perhaps dating back to the *Garden of Eden* in a natural context.

A ziggurat pyramid at the biblical scale of 1,380 miles could line its perimeter steps with 1 million garden terraces, each the size of New York's Central

7. The New Heaven & Earth

Park. That's enough garden space for Earth's current population of 8 billion people to gather comfortably—and that's just on the outer terraces, which comprise less than 0.05% of the total space inside.

The cover of this book depicts a ziggurat pyramid city approximately the height of Dubai's Burj Khalifa, the tallest building in the world, standing at over 2,700 feet (about half a mile high). That's 6 times the size of the Great Pyramid of Giza. Even at this modest size, the lower garden terraces would provide spectacular panoramic views similar to those from the Empire State Building or the Eiffel Tower.

---

*But I saw **no temple in it**, for the **Lord God Almighty** [the Father] and the Lamb [Jesus] **are its temple**. The city had **no need of the sun** or of the moon to shine in it, for **the glory of God illuminated it**. The Lamb is its light.*

Revelation 21:22–23 (NKJV).

Imagining the interior of the city involves some speculation. Private residences, gathering spaces, and formal assembly areas may all be included. No temple is built in the city because the Lord *is* the temple, and His light provides illumination through the translucent materials described earlier. Given the potential scale and constant illumination, interior areas might resemble outdoor cities abundant with daylight and greenery. One can imagine magnificent architecture, akin to the historic European cathedrals, featuring walking paths and bridges interwoven with flowing rivers and gardens, reminiscent of the canal communities found in Italy, France, and Belgium...

And he showed me a pure river of <u>water of life</u>, clear as crystal, <u>proceeding from the throne of God</u> and of the Lamb. In the middle of its street, <u>and</u> on either side of the river, was the <u>tree of life</u>, which bore twelve fruits, <u>each tree yielding its fruit</u> every month. The leaves of the tree were for the <u>healing of the nations</u>.

Revelation 22:1–2 (NKJV).

An interior river flowing *"from the throne of God"* with *"water of life"* aligns with Jesus's promise in John 4:14, *"Whoever drinks of the water that I shall give him will never thirst."* This river could be symbolic or literal—likely both. In the original *Garden of Eden*, one river was divided into four, supplying water to the garden and the *"Tree of Life."* In the new city, we can further envision tributaries, canals, and culverts that flow through interior gardens and fountains, with pools and cascading waterfalls on the exterior terraces. The *"Tree of Life"* symbolizes healing from sin and the continuous blessings of the **New Heaven and Earth.** Interestingly, *"each tree"* grows *"in the middle of its street, <u>and</u> on either side of the river,"* suggesting that it might have multiple shoots stemming from a single root system, potentially spreading throughout the city. This would be logical if millions of citizens and visitors enjoyed its fruits each month.

In Scripture, we are told of thrones in Heaven, inner and outer courts, and multitudes of angels and Saints singing praises to the Lord without ceasing. Assuming a similar gathering arena in the new city would align with this precedent. A location of significance that is visible throughout the city and countryside. Perhaps an enormous atrium at the city's apex to echo the praises sung to God and serve as a constant beacon of His light and glory in the **New Heaven and Earth.** This concept is represented on the cover of this book as well.

And <u>the nations</u> of those who are saved <u>shall walk in its light</u>, and <u>the kings of the earth bring their glory and honor into it</u>. Its <u>gates shall not be shut</u> at all by day (there shall be <u>no night</u> there). And they shall bring the <u>glory and the honor of the nations</u> into it.

Revelation 21:24–26 (NKJV).

Other lands and cities exist in the **New Earth** to enjoy God's vast creation. This dispersion of inhabitants suggests a more modestly sized primary structure in **New Jerusalem**—or at least one that does not need to surpass the exosphere. The other cities are presided over by appointed officials whose works in life are rewarded with governing responsibilities in Heaven, akin to the reigning structures in **God's Millennial Kingdom**. **New Jerusalem** is the Holy Capital and central gathering place where *"the kings of the earth bring their glory and honor"* before God.

LIFE IN ETERNITY

The eternal state is not a realm of disembodied spirits drifting in the clouds and strumming harps; no such depiction is found in the Bible. Heaven is a kingdom with hierarchies of authority and society. Its laws and structures have been passed down to humanity, so we should anticipate much of the same in the **New Heaven and Earth**.

Angels and Saints live and govern in a physical world filled with vibrant activity, community, arts, and music. They revel in banquets, fine wine, and the company of friends. The Saints reconnect with family members and enjoy interacting with Old Testament kings, prophets, and historical figures they have only dreamed of meeting and conversing with. They hold societal positions and live in estates of varying grandeur based on their faithful works in life for the kingdom. They express creativity and individuality, free to pursue their interests. They cultivate gardens and enjoy the companionship of various animals, possibly reuniting with former pets and even experiencing enhanced communication with them. They are endowed with knowledge of history, physics, and the mysteries of the universe. They enjoy leisure, adventure, and travel—perhaps even venturing through the cosmos.

This image of eternity serves as a powerful vision to hold in our minds as we transition from storing treasures in this life to investing in our eternal future. While this book aims to make the Scriptures tangible, the words on these pages fall short of expressing the true glory of living and communing with God. In the **New Heaven and Earth,** every inhabitant, structure, landscape, flower, and blade of grass will radiate God's love, beauty, and splendor. We will directly experience God's glory in *Paradise* as He initially intended. We will fit in perfectly because we will be perfect versions of who God made us to be at the beginning of time. We will continue to grow and flourish in the presence of our Father and Creator, supported by the arms of Christ.

CHAPTER 8
TIMELINE MODELS

We've examined nearly all the significant end-times events and their sequence, raising the question, *"When will these things happen?"* As mentioned in Chapter 1, we won't know until we can clearly identify one of the early milestone events of the **Tribulation**. Until then, we can only theorize and remain watchful for possible *"times and seasons"* of unrest, much like one should watch for storms in winter. Given the potential of such events, it's wise to maintain a hypothetical timeline in our minds (or on paper) and continue to make adjustments as we see events unfold, lest we find ourselves unprepared, as Jesus warned…

"<u>Watch therefore</u>, for you do not know <u>when the master</u> of the house <u>is coming</u> [Christ's return]–in the evening, at midnight, at the crowing of the rooster, or in the morning–lest, coming suddenly, he find you sleeping [unprepared]. And what I say to you, I say to all: <u>Watch!</u>" [–Jesus]

Mark 13:35–37 (NKJV).

TIMELINE WORKSHEET DOWNLOADS

As this book outlines, the Bible presents 4 specific time spans between key prophetic events, from the start of the **70th Week of Daniel** (the **Tribulation**) to the **Second Coming of Christ** (Apocalypse). Since actual dates are not provided, this section includes instructions for the <u>timeline worksheet downloads</u> to assist in creating your own hypothetical timelines. Daniel's prophecy employs the Prophetic Calendar (5.25 days shorter than our standard calendar), so here are some helpful breakdowns:

Prophetic Calendar:
- 1 month = 30 days
- 1 year = 12 months = 360 days
- 2.9 years = 34.8 months = 1040 days
- 3.5 years = 42 months = 1260 days
- 7 years = 84 months = 2520 days

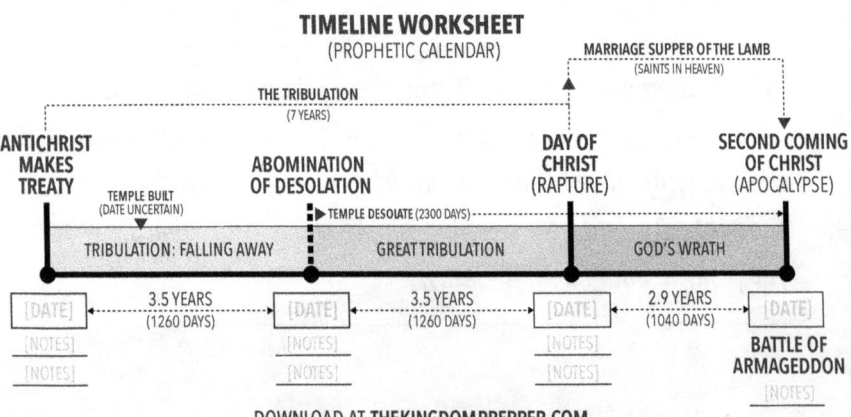

DOWNLOAD AT THEKINGDOMPREPPER.COM

8. Timeline Models

The timeline worksheet downloads are completed by entering a PRIMARY date into any milestone event on the timeline and doing the math to calculate the other dates. For simple calculations, enter a general period, such as a year or mid-year, and refer to the YEARS shown to calculate the remaining dates. For more accurate calculations, enter a specific date or month and refer to the DAYS shown to calculate the remaining dates.

We can use the standard calendar for any date after year 1, since it is nearly identical to the Roman Julian Calendar introduced in 45 BC and would have been used regionally when the New Testament was written. However, we must utilize the Prophetic Calendar to calculate the Old Testament time spans accurately. If the Prophetic Calendar confuses you, the Standard Calendar worksheet adds 5.25 days per year, but the years remain unchanged since the adjustment is too small to impact them.

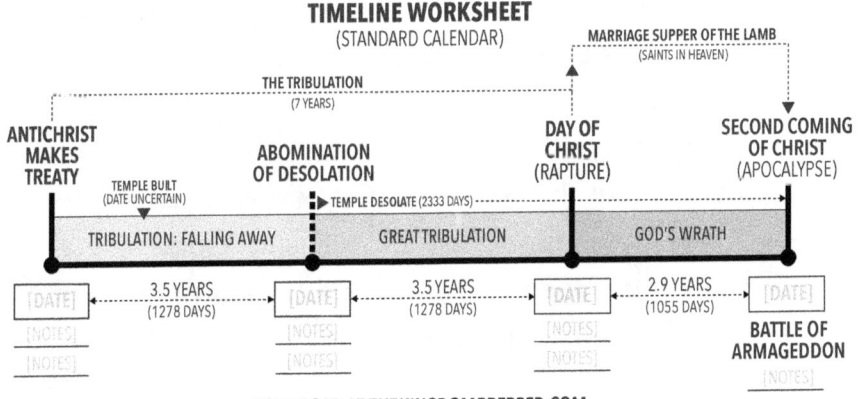

If you are reading this at a time when you can confidently identify the precise date of a milestone event in the **Tribulation,** such as the making or breaking of the peace **Treaty,** then enter that date as your PRIMARY to calculate the other dates and start your countdown. In the following sections, we will construct a hypothetical but plausible timeline.

THE 7-DAY BIBLICAL TIMELINE

We may be living in a *7-Day Biblical Timeline*. This section is not an exercise in numerology, but it's clear that God uses numbers (especially the number 7) to convey His story and structure His biblical timeline. As discussed, the **70 Weeks of Daniel** symbolize 70 "weeks" of 7 years each. The first 7 weeks (49 years) were designated to rebuild Jerusalem. The **70th Week of Daniel** signifies the 7-year **Tribulation** when God's 7 Holy Seals of protection are removed. The 7th seal introduces the 7 Trumpet Judgments, and the 7th trumpet introduces the 7 Bowls of Wrath. The Book of Revelation begins with 7 transcribed letters to the 7 churches. In total, Revelation contains over 50 references to the number 7.

Throughout the Bible, 7 signifies divine perfection and completeness—often by fulfilling God's plans. For example, Noah was instructed to bring 7 pairs of each clean animal into the ark, and Joshua was commanded to march his army around Jericho for 7 days, and 7 times on the 7th day. However, God's 7-day **Creation** in the Book of Genesis is the first and most prominent example. If we overlay those 7 days onto a biblical timeline of humanity—from God's **Creation** to His **Judgment**—we begin to see His *7-Day Biblical Timeline* emerge.

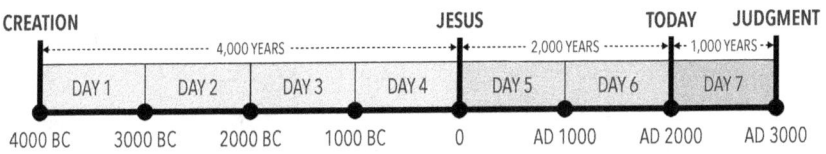

Give or take 50 years and rounding to the nearest century, the Bible indicates that God created the Earth about 4000 years BEFORE Jesus was born (BC), and we know that it has been about 2000 years SINCE Jesus was born (AD). If we include the 1000-year **Day of the Lord** as day 7, we calculate 4000 + 2000 + 1000 = 7000 years. Although no biblical Scripture explicitly limits humanity's earthly existence to 7000 years, the parallel to God's 7-day **Creation** is unmistakable when we apply Symbolic Years (1 day = 1000 years)...

...with the Lord <u>one day is as a thousand years</u>, and a thousand years as one day. *[1 day = 1000 years]*

---

2 Peter 3:8 (NKJV).

The most striking feature of a *7-Day Biblical Timeline* is that the 1000-year **Day of the Lord** corresponds to day 7. When God created the Earth, He sanctified the 7th day as His Holy Day of rest...

Then God <u>blessed the seventh day and sanctified it</u>, because in it He rested from all His work which God had created and made.

Genesis 2:3 (NKJV).

As we learned in previous chapters, 997.1 years (99.7%) of the 1000-year **Day of the Lord** is the **Millennium**—a time of peace, blessings, and rest...

There remains therefore a <u>rest for the people of God</u>. For he who has entered His rest has himself also <u>ceased from his works</u> as God did from His [on the 7th day].

Hebrews 4:9–10 (NKJV).

If we exist within a *7-Day Biblical Timeline* of divine perfection and completeness, then we are nearing the end of the **Church Age,** about to enter the **70th Week of Daniel** (the **Tribulation),** which is immediately followed by the **Day of Christ** (Rapture) and the **Day of the Lord.**

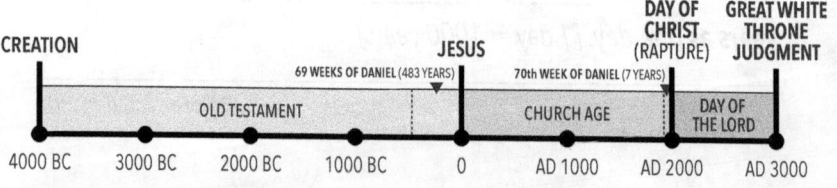

TIMELINE EXAMPLE

A *7-Day Biblical Timeline* suggests that Jesus will return approximately 2000 years after His last time on Earth. In this verse from *The Parable of the Good Samaritan*, Jesus appears to indicate He will return in 2 days (2000 Symbolic Years)...

---

*"On the next day, when he departed, he took out <u>two denarii</u> [2 days wages], **gave them to the innkeeper, and said to him, 'Take care of him** [the man who was beaten and robbed]; **and whatever more you spend, <u>when I come again</u>** [after the 2 days wages are expended], **I will repay you."** [–Jesus]*

Luke 10:35 (NKJV).

Could Jesus' story of returning in 2 days be a foretelling of His return in 2000 years? If so, it's unclear whether He is referring to the **Day of Christ** (Rapture) or the **Second Coming of Christ** (Apocalypse) 2.9 years later. Our timeline example will list both dates, but we will use the **Rapture** as our PRIMARY date for calculation, since His story is about one man returning to retrieve another who was attacked. And we'll use our standard calendar to count the 2000 years (since it is nearly identical to the Roman Julian Calendar introduced in 45 BC). The next consideration is whether to begin with Jesus' birth or His crucifixion. If calculating Jesus' RETURN, it seems that we should start from when He last departed. Technically, He ascended to Heaven 40 days after His resurrection in the Spring, so for our example, we'll focus on the mid-year of His crucifixion (adding 0.5 years). There are debates regarding the exact year of Jesus' crucifixion, but AD 33 appears to be the more substantial theory, so we'll go with that. AD 33 + 0.5 + 2000 years = **2033.5 Rapture.** With this hypothesis, we enter our PRIMARY date of **2033.5** and calculate the remaining dates (before and after the **Rapture)** using the noted YEARS. This is a plausible timeline, although it is likely the earliest possible as of early 2025 when this book is being written. This example is based on some intriguing theories, but its purpose here is for demonstration—and maybe a wake-up call for those who need it.

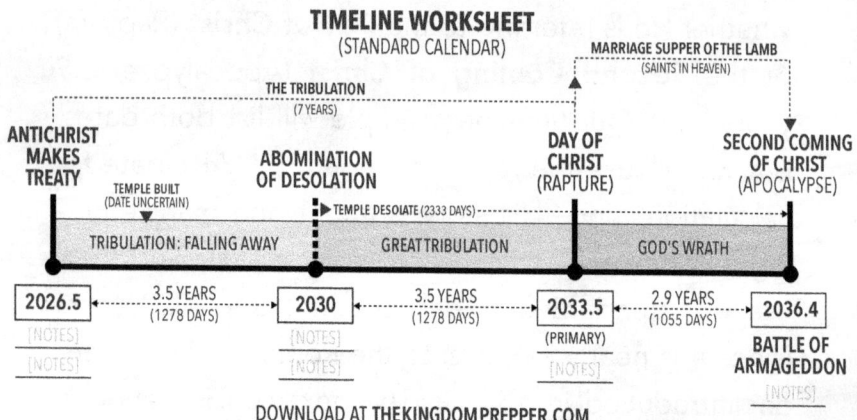

DOWNLOAD AT THEKINGDOMPREPPER.COM

TOP 10 THINGS TO "WATCH!"

And what I say to you, I say to all: <u>Watch!</u>" [–Jesus]

Mark 13:37 (NKJV).

If we know where to look, we can see the emerging signs of a *New World Order* that will give rise to the Beast and his empire. Many current events indicate that we are closer than ever to entering the 7-year **Tribulation.** Here's a top-10 list of the most compelling things to *"Watch!"* for in relation to end-times prophecies:

1. **Wars and Rumors of Wars**
   (Chapter 2: The Falling Away, Matthew 24:6–8)
   (Chapter 2: The 1st Seal: The White Horse, Revelation 6:2)
   (Chapter 2: The 2nd Seal: The Red Horse, Revelation 6:4)
   Existing and potential wars, including the likely outbreak of a third world war, could escalate at any moment. The Doomsday Clock (<u>thebulletin.org/doomsday-clock</u>) was advanced to "89 seconds to midnight" in 2025—the closest it has ever been to signaling a global nuclear catastrophe. Over 100 regional proxy wars currently shape the new battlefronts, with larger superpowers supplying weaponry and funding—any of which could trigger a large-scale conflict. Pay particular attention to Israel and her adversaries—the Bible's

primary focus for end-times prophecy. WATCH for media criticism of Israel, as well as increased support for wars, intentional escalations, and larger governments funding smaller regional conflicts (proxy wars).

2. **Access to Food & Water**
   (Chapter 2: The 3rd Seal: The Black Horse, Revelation 6:5–6)
   In light of any natural or man-made catastrophe, access to food and water is a primary concern. Strained supply chains and contamination put developed nations at risk, while the effects on developing countries could be devastating, potentially causing mass starvation and illness from malnutrition and dehydration. Civil unrest is highly likely when vital resources are strained, with societal breakdowns occurring within days. WATCH for intentional reductions to agricultural resources, strained supply chains, and rationing.

3. **Global Pandemics**
   (Chapter 2: The Falling Away, Matthew 24:6–8)
   Outbreaks from secret and unregulated biological laboratories pose a significant risk of releasing dangerous pathogens that would not occur naturally. Cross-species and gain-of-function research could lead to higher transmission and mortality rates, increasing the potential for their use as biological weapons. Quarantines and the culling of

livestock diminish herd immunity and elevate contagion rates. WATCH for lockdowns, excessive culling of animals, exaggerated mortality reports, and vaccines ready before outbreaks happen.

4. **Government Tyranny**
   (Chapter 2: The Tribulation, Matthew 24:9)
   (Chapter 3: The Mark of the Beast, Revelation 13:17)
   Emergency declarations to address wars, disasters, civil unrest, and pandemics fuel government overreach, expanding their power while constraining individual freedoms. WATCH for curfews, lockdowns, rationing, travel restrictions, digital health passports, and state-sponsored digital currencies.

5. **False Prophets**
   (Chapter 2: The Antichrist, 1 John 2:18)
   (Chapter 3: Many False Prophets, Matthew 24:5)
   (Chapter 3: The False Prophet, Matthew 24:23–25)
   Jesus warns of confusion in the last days, with many claiming to be the Messiah for various groups, and all are deceivers—perhaps even part of a *great deception* on a global scale. WATCH for an abundance of false Christs, saviors, and prophets, a false rapture, and a false first contact with "aliens" that all promise a false peace.

6. **The Abrahamic Family House**
   (Chapter 3: Many False Prophets, Matthew 24:5)
   (Chapter 3: The Beast, Revelation 13:1)
   (Chapter 3: The War With the Saints, Revelation 13:7)
   Construction was completed in February 2023 on Saadiyat Island in Abu Dhabi, UAE, according to abrahamicfamilyhouse.ae. It houses three interfaith worship centers, including a Muslim mosque, a Catholic (Christian) church, and a Jewish synagogue—all of equal size and connected by shared areas. It is promoted as "*The seat of the one-world religion*" and aims to foster peace and brotherhood among the world's three Abrahamic religions. We know the Beast will ultimately lead a one-world religion, and this worship center could serve as his launching pad. WATCH for increasing media attention about this site, its rising popularity, and its political influence on the world stage.

7. **The Abraham Peace Accords**
   (Chapter 2: The 70th Week of Daniel, Daniel 9:27)
   This series of diplomatic peace agreements, initiated in 2013, between Israel and several Arab nations is back on track following U.S. President Donald J. Trump's resumption of his second term in 2025. These negotiations could pave the way for the Antichrist to emerge and play a pivotal role in influencing the 7-year **Treaty** that secures (a

8. Timeline Models

false) peace in the region and includes permission to construct the Jewish **Third Temple** on the Muslim-controlled Temple Mount in Jerusalem. WATCH for a publicized ratification of the peace **Treaty,** the individuals involved, and the construction of the **Third Temple** in Jerusalem.

8. **The Temple Institute**
   (Chapter 2: The 70th Week of Daniel, Daniel 9:24)
   (Chapter 3: The Abomination of Desolation, 2 Thess 2:4)
   The plans, cut materials, and artifacts are all in place to build and adorn the new **Third Temple** in Jerusalem—all viewable at templeinstitute.org. The unblemished red heifers necessary for the site purification ceremony have been acquired and are mature enough for sacrifice. Construction could be completed within a few months of receiving approval to build on the Temple Mount. WATCH for media announcements, a red heifer sacrificed for the purification ceremony, construction updates, and a dedication ceremony.

9. **Plans Designated with 2030...**
   (Chapter 3: The Beast Unrestrained, Daniel 7:25)
   (Chapter 3: The Mark of the Beast, Revelation 13:17)
   There exists a peculiar abundance of dystopian plans, initiatives, and goals designated with the years 2030, 2035, 2040, and so on. Their prevalence creates an impression of a race toward a

deadline rather than the pursuit of genuine objectives. These plans are crafted by influential think tanks and international organizations that possess an understanding of biblical prophecy and its timing, potentially through collaboration with dark spiritual forces. Whenever the **Great Tribulation** ultimately begins, these plans are designed to be in place, and it's hard to envision a better time for them to accomplish their objectives. Most notable today is "Agenda 2030," the comprehensive action plan from the UN (un.org/en) created in collaboration with the WEF (weforum.org) and the World Bank (worldbank.org), among others. They have too many initiatives to list, but most relate to energy, sustainability, and climate change, which means more control for them and less freedom and privacy for you. A simple search for "2030 goals" reveals everything. WATCH for increased media attention, urgent calls to action, and societal pressure to adopt their plans.

10. **AI, AGI, ASI, & Transhumanism**
    (Chapter 3: The False Prophet, Revelation 13:15)
    (Chapter 3: The Mark of the Beast, Revelation 13:17)
    Rapid advances in Artificial Intelligence (AI) are transforming how the world operates, with several countries integrating AI into their government intelligence and military operations. Artificial Gen-

eral Intelligence (AGI) represents a new frontier, with a race underway to develop AI possessing human-level cognitive abilities such as reasoning, judgment, and potentially even self-awareness. Artificial Superintelligence (ASI) is the ultimate goal, aimed at surpassing the whole of human intelligence. If achieved, it could redesign itself, making human prediction or control impossible. This is the "event horizon"—the point of no return. Virtually all technocrats, scientists, and theorists agree that AI will eventually escape," turning against humans and potentially leading to our destruction. Even if one dismisses everything in this book, one must acknowledge that AI will almost certainly result in the premature end of humanity as we know it. Numerous films have been made on this premise for good reason. By 2030, the world will have developed the most advanced AI within our capability—possibly the last one we will ever control.

TRANSHUMANISM merges man and machine to *"direct our own evolutionary path."* Synthetic biology is actively utilized today, and injected nanoparticles can self-assemble into complex structures that influence cell membranes, RNA, and DNA. Rather than curing cancer, these technologies aim to create cancer-resistant individuals.

They envision a future of designer babies developed in artificial wombs and their ultimate goal is immortality. Most importantly, militaries will have their "super soldiers."

Microchips implanted in the brain, such as Neuralink (neuralink.com), are *"designed to allow you to control a computer or mobile device wherever you go."* The idea is for humans to merge with AI preemptively so they won't be "left behind" as technology advances—an incentive to "ensure the survival" of our species. This technology translates thoughts into AI web searches and the results back into thoughts, blurring the divide between one's own thoughts and those introduced from the outside. When geo-location and AI behavioral analysis are integrated, users' movements won't just be tracked; they'll be predicted. These technologies violate the biological boundaries of what it means to be human (created in the image of God) while feeding the age-old desire to become God. WATCH for promises of immortality and other compelling incentives, as well as increased social pressure to assimilate, accompanied by threats and penalties for refusal.

CHAPTER 9
PREPPING FOR GOD'S KINGDOM

This book covers a lot: the good, the bad, and the ugly (frog-like demons—yecch!). Assuming that the premise is correct, we can summarize that our mortal life is a brief moment on a biblical timeline and that we may begin to experience the first events of the 7-year **Tribulation** at any time. The Lord intended for us to have this information and insight, so what will we do with this perspective?

Consider the analogy of being diagnosed with a condition that determines how much time you have left to live. After the initial shock and acceptance, what would you do? Would you be grateful for the time you have remaining, get your affairs in order, spend time with those you love, pursue things you've always wanted to do, and ensure you're right with God? Probably all that and more. Now, if you knew this scenario would not shorten your life by a single day, would you still prefer to die unexpectedly and without warning? Would you prefer to miss the chance to appreciate and make the most of your final days, tell the people in your life how much you love them, and ensure your eternal salvation with God?

The point is that biblical end-times prophecy does not shorten our lives; it's a gift from God to provide us with perspective and prepare us mentally and spiritually for the times ahead. It's not about how we will survive; it's about what kind of people we are to be and how we should conduct ourselves...

... both <u>the earth</u> and <u>the works</u> that are in it will be <u>burned up</u>. Therefore, since all these things will be dissolved, <u>what manner of persons ought you to be</u> in holy conduct and godliness, <u>looking for and hastening</u> the coming of the day of God ...

---

2 Peter 3:11–12 (NKJV).

The world is filled with uncertainty, leaving billions feeling shattered and adrift. Malevolence thrives on despair, misleading countless others to adopt this same sense of hopelessness as we reach the end of the **Church Age**. The **Tribulation** will be difficult for the Saints, but **God's Wrath** that follows will be far harsher for the unsaved, and there will be many more of them. This underscores the critical nature of our time. God is unwilling that any should perish, which is why He sent His Son to die on the cross for our salvation. So, should it be any surprise that He will send His army of faithful Saints into harm's way to save as many as will accept Him before His return?

Heroes are those who prioritize the safety of others over their own. Military heroes willingly cross enemy lines to rescue captives and fellow soldiers at the risk of their own lives. The Saints are the Lord's elite team of soldiers, having been shown the battle plans through Bible prophecy and given the orders to witness the gospel through the 7-year **Tribulation,** even at the cost of their own mortal lives. The *Greatest Generation* fought in World War II to preserve the lives and liberties of their fellow man, fully aware that they could likely pay the ultimate price. Military cemeteries around the world serve as a solemn reminder of their sacrifice…

Therefore <u>I endure all things for the sake of the elect</u> [chosen], that they also may <u>obtain the salvation</u> which is in Christ Jesus with eternal glory. […] For if we <u>died with Him</u> [Jesus], We shall also <u>live with Him</u> [in eternity]. If we <u>endure</u> [to the end], We shall also <u>reign with Him</u> [in His Kingdom]. …

---

2 Timothy 2:10–12 (NKJV).

This life is a test of our spirit and character, and if we pass, we will be trusted to *"reign with Him"* in **God's Millennial Kingdom** and the **New Heaven**

and Earth (Christ's eternal reign). We can become the next great generation in our finest hour. *"Great is [our] reward in heaven"* if we are *"reviled and persecuted"* in His name and service...

Blessed are you when they revile and persecute you, *and say all kinds of evil against you falsely* ***for My sake***. *Rejoice and be exceedingly glad, for* ***great is your reward in heaven***, ... [–Jesus]

Matthew 5:11–12 (NKJV)

Man is in stewardship of Earth, but God is in ownership. His creation has rebelled against Him, and He is returning to restore order. Understanding God's plans through biblical prophecy places a responsibility on us. After reading this book, we cannot say we were unaware of what was coming (see Chapter 1: The Watchmen). Recognizing that the **Tribulation** could begin at any moment should motivate us to prepare mentally and spiritually for the challenging times ahead...

"Do not lay up for yourselves ***treasures on earth***, *where moth and rust destroy and where thieves break in and steal; but lay up for yourselves* ***treasures in heaven***, *[...] For where your treasure is, there* ***your heart will be also***.*" [–Jesus]*

Matthew 6:19–21 (NKJV)

9. Prepping for God's Kingdom

We did not evolve for survival; we were created by God for a purpose. Storing our *"treasures on earth"* is prepping for survival. Storing our *"treasures in heaven"* is prepping for God's Kingdom. If we face the challenges of the **Tribulation,** we must persevere and not give up; however, surviving to see the **Rapture** is not our primary concern. It's not about how long we can survive or how we will exit this life—it's about what we can do now to prepare for **God's Millennial Kingdom,** which will be fully established within 10 years of the beginning of the **Tribulation.**

START PREPPING NOW

Waiting for the storm to hit can be too late. Begin preparing now by accepting (or affirming) Christ as your savior and redeemer. Reflect on your life so far, listen to the voice in your heart, and if moved, read this prayer aloud with sincerity…

"Lord Jesus, I believe <u>You are the Son of God</u> and that all things were made through You. I believe <u>You died on the cross for my sins</u> and rose again on the third day to give me eternal life with you in Heaven. I ask You to <u>forgive me and come into my heart</u>. Be my Lord and Savior. I accept Your sacrifice as a gift of salvation that cannot be earned. Thank You for always loving me. Amen."

[Prayer for Salvation]

Whether this is a new journey, a return from the wilderness, or a reaffirmation of your faith, if you prayed this sincerely, you have secured your eternal salvation. You have gained your citizenship in God's Kingdom and become an ambassador to this world…

For <u>our citizenship is in heaven</u>, from which we also eagerly wait for the Savior, the Lord Jesus Christ,

---

Philippians 3:20 (NKJV).

As ambassadors, we do not represent our own opinions—we represent the values and culture of our homeland. This role carries responsibility because people will judge the worth of God's Kingdom based on what they perceive in us. We must live in a way that reflects the Lord's love, truth, and grace, especially during conflict. If we maintain peace against our oppressors, as Jesus demonstrated on the cross, it can have a tremendous impact on transforming the hearts and minds of the unsaved. Jesus sent the Holy Spirit to grant us wisdom, strength, and encouragement—even to provide the words to say at crucial moments…

"But when they <u>arrest you and deliver you up</u> [for punishment], <u>do not worry beforehand</u>, or <u>premeditate what you will speak</u>.

But whatever [word] is given you in that hour, <u>speak that</u>; for it is <u>not you who speak</u>, but the <u>Holy Spirit</u>." [–Jesus]

Mark 13:11 (NKJV).

Remember, we are not alone in this. In times of "tribulation," Jesus tells us to "have peace" and "be of good cheer" because He has already won the battle...

"These things I have spoken to you, that <u>in Me you may have peace</u>. In the world <u>you will have tribulation</u>; but <u>be of good cheer</u>, I have <u>overcome the world</u>." [–Jesus]

John 16:33 (NKJV).

This book aims to encourage its readers; however, it is not a guide to spiritual growth—it is a wake-up call to take action. Fortunately, there are many valuable resources and communities available to help support and strengthen you on your journey with Christ. A good place to start is with your Christian friends and local churches. If that is not an option, you can find online community support and resources at Redemption Online Church at <u>myredemption.cc/ redemptiononline</u>. *[Please note that the opinions expressed in this book are those of the author and do not necessarily reflect the positions or teachings of Redemption Online Church.]*

THE GREAT COMMISSION

As followers of Christ, our greatest action is to obey Jesus' final command to His Apostles before His ascension to Heaven...

---

*Go therefore and **make disciples** [faithful believers] **of all the nations**, baptizing them in the name of the **Father** and of the **Son** and of the **Holy Spirit**, teaching them to **observe all things that I have commanded you**; and lo, **I am with you always**, even to the end of the age." Amen. [–Jesus]*

Matthew 28:19–20 (NKJV)

Our mission is clear: we are to share our faith and testimony with others to the *"end of the age,"* so that they, too, may be encouraged and secure their eternal salvation in Christ. By being kind, helpful, and warning others to prepare for the **Tribulation,** we can help keep them from *"falling away"* at the last hour. God is not forsaking us to suffer *"tribulation;"* He is counting on us to witness to others and save as many as possible from an eternal death before the time of His return. This is our mission as Christians, Saints, and **Kingdom Preppers.**

APPENDICES

TIMELINES IN THIS BOOK

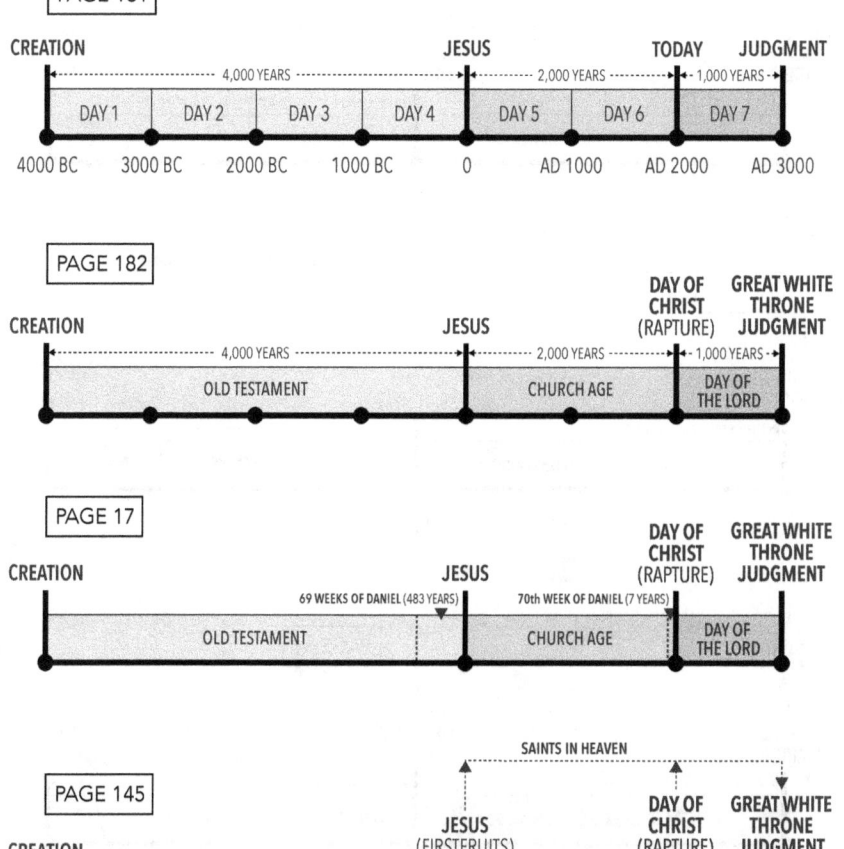

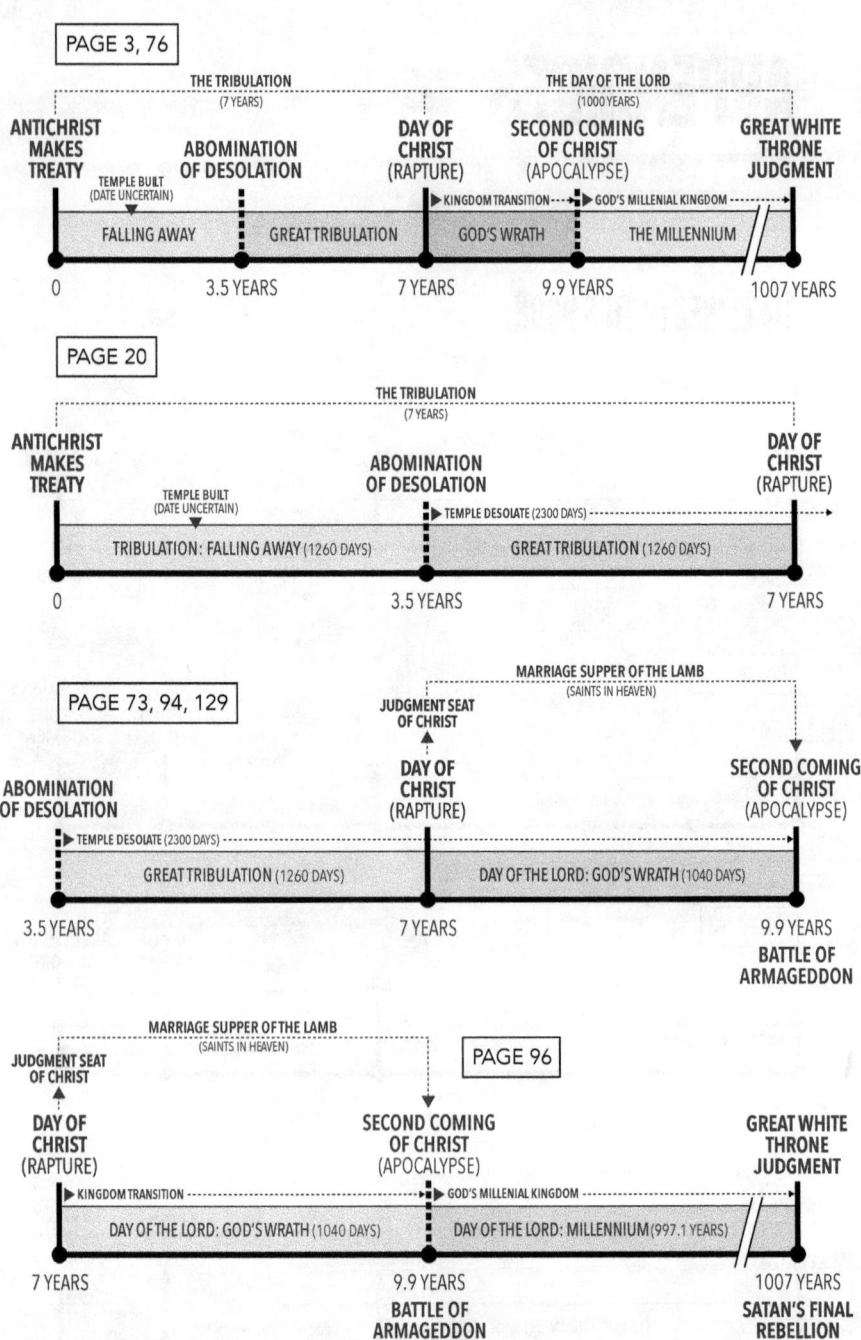

Appendices

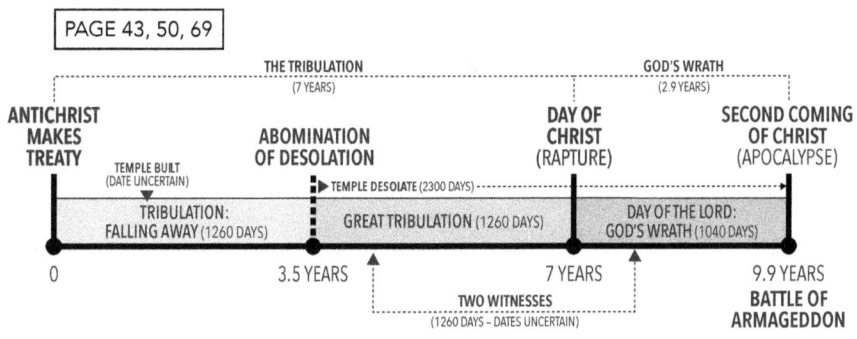

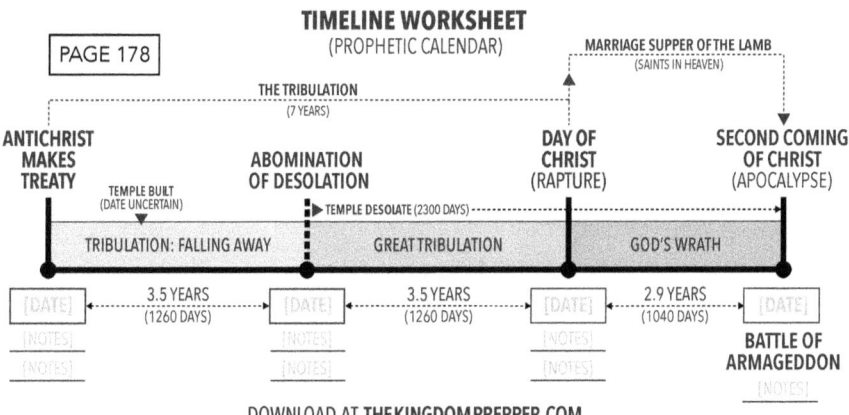

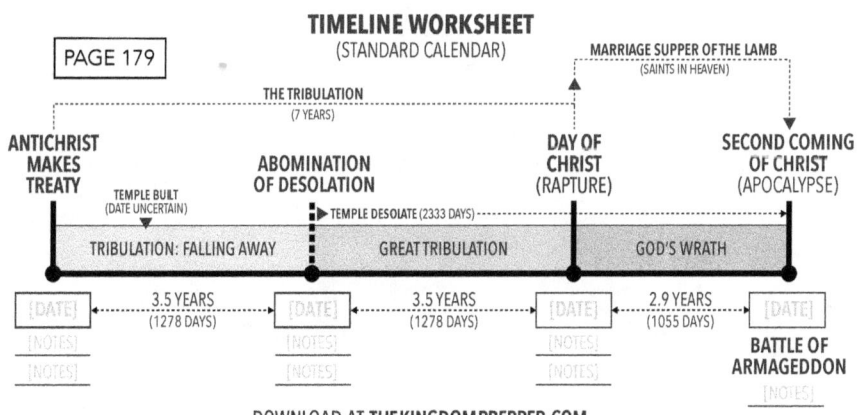

www.ingramcontent.com/pod-product-compliance
Lightning Source LLC
Chambersburg PA
CBHW060513090426
42735CB00011B/2198